Cruising Designs
POWER AND SAIL
By Edward S. Brewer

In Association
with
Robert E. Wallstrom

Seven Seas Press, New York, N.Y.

To those professionals who
taught us all we know:
George Cuthbertson
Bill Luders
Phil Rhodes
John Atkin

*ACKNOWLEDGMENT: The authors wish to express
their appreciation to the editors of Sail Magazine for
their permission to reprint "The Sailing Auxiliary."*

Brewer, Edward S.
   Cruising designs: power and sail—by Edward S.
Brewer, in association with Robert E. Wallstrom.—
1st ed.—New York: Seven Seas Press, ©1976.
144 p.ill.; 23 cm.

ISBN 0-915160-15-3
LIBRARY OF CONGRESS CATALOG NO. 76-360654

   1. Yacht-building—Designs and plans. I. Wallstrom,
Robert E., joint author. II. Title.

©1976, SEVEN SEAS PRESS
FIRST EDITION
SECOND PRINTING, 1977

PRINTED IN THE UNITED STATES OF AMERICA

Contents

ABOUT THE DESIGNERS:
  Edward S. Brewer 4
  Robert E. Wallstrom 5
PREFACE 6
THE CRUISING AUXILIARY:
  Trends in Hull Design 7
  Performance And The Cruising Boat 14
  Selecting A Design 19
  Layout And Performance 23
  Obtaining Proper Balance 28
  Power Plants And Auxiliary Sailboats 32
CRUISING AUXILIARY DESIGNS:
  20-Ft. Sloop *Phialle* 36
  21-Ft. Catboat *Cape Cod* 38
  22-Ft. Ketch *Grand Banks 22* 42
  25-Ft. Catboat *Chappaquiddick* 45
  26-Ft. Eastport Pinky *Albert Hallet* 48
  28-Ft. Sloop *Aloha 28* 52
  28-Ft. Ketch *Grand Banks 28* 54
  30-Ft. Ketch *Carib* 57
  32-Ft. Schooner *Lazyjack* 59
  32-Ft. Sloop *Douglas 32* 61
  32-Ft. Ketch *Tern* 64
  32-Ft. Sharpie Ketch *Mystic* 67
  33-Ft. Staysail Schooner *Ingenue* 70
  34-Ft. Sloop *Aloha* 73
  34-Ft. Pinky Sloop *Sunshine* 75
  35-Ft. Cutter *Jason* 77
  35-Ft. Cutter *MB/S 35* 80
  36-Ft. Sloop/Cutter *Cabot 36* 83
  36-Ft. Ketch *Amee* 85
  38-Ft. Friendship Sloop 87
  42-Ft. Ketch *Whitby 42* 90
  43-Ft. Cutter *Black Velvet II* 93
  43-Ft. Yawl *Cape North* 97
  43-Ft. Ketch *Pacific 42* 99
  44-Ft. Ketch *Cape Race* 101
  45-Ft. Pinky Schooner (after *Dove*) 104
  47-Ft. Ketch *Olympic Adventure* 107
  51-Ft. Yawl *Julie* 110
  54-Ft. Ketch *Enterprise* 112
  56-Ft. Schooner *Mystic* 115
  61-Ft. Ketch *Traveller* III 119
A PORTFOLIO OF BREWER BOATS 119
POWERBOATS:
  18-Ft. Outboard Cruiser *Herrick Bay 18* 124
  20-Ft. Outboard Cruiser *Herrick Bay 20* 125
  24-Ft. Sport/Day Cruiser *Flye Point 24* 126
  27-Ft. Weekend Cruiser *Blue Hill* 128
  28-Ft. Cruiser *Deer Isle 28* 130
  32-Ft. Cruiser *Dragon Lady* 133
  33-Ft. Cruiser *Grand Banks 33* 135
  37-Ft. Cruiser *Deer Isle 37* 139

About The Designers

Ted Brewer was born in Canada 42 years ago, and says, "I am a Canuck still." As a boy of 12 he joined the Canadian Sea Cadets where he learned to sail in 14-foot dinghies and 27-foot whaleboats. His father was in the Canadian Navy and Ted planned the same career for himself, "but I failed the eye test," he says, "and chose the army instead." Ted began to study yacht design while doing his army hitch. Then in 1957 he went to work for George Cuthbertson as a yacht broker. In 1960 he came to the U.S. to join Bill Luders as an assistant designer, working on *Weatherly, American Eagle,* dozens of 5.5-meter sloops, and many other boats.

In 1967 he moved to Brooklin, Maine, and started his own design business. Then in 1968, with Jim Betts, he founded the Yacht Design Institute which offers correspondence courses in yacht design, and that operation is still going strong—now with Bob Wallstrom as his partner in this venture.

As for cruising and racing, he has had a large measure of it. In 1969 and 1973 he raced in the Transpac aboard his own design, the 55-foot ketch *Mystic,* taking a 2nd in Class B in 1969. From 1960 through 1967 he raced with Bill Luders aboard Luders' 39-foot *Storm* in many Long Island Sound races. He has also raced in "a dozen or more" distance races such as Monhegan, Newport-Annapolis and S.O.R.C., besides making a 1964 yacht delivery cruise to Bermuda."

Ted is a member of S.N.A.M.E., S.S.C.D., N.A.M.S., and is a technical member of A.B.Y.C. He is, as well, Design Editor of Motor Boating & Sailing magazine, writing the design commentaries for that publication each month. He is the author of *Understanding Boat Design,* a book used as a text in the Yacht Design Institute, and is an occasional contributor—as much as his busy schedule permits—to several boating magazines.

Although his schedule of design work does not permit him as much cruising as he would like, he goes off on short cruises aboard his 22-foot Drascombe Longboat. For Ted Brewer, "Open boat cruising is the way to go."

Bob Wallstrom is 41, an American, and is married and has two children. His yacht design experience began in 1964 with the Luders organization, where he worked first as a draftsman and in the mold loft, then as an assistant designer on the *American Eagle* program. After leaving Luders he worked for several years in the design office of Philip Rhodes, as draftsman, and on one major project, designing the 123-foot, 3 masted steel schooner, *Sea Star*.

In 1969, Bob moved to Brooklin, Maine, to join Ted Brewer as a partner in the design business. Shortly afterwards, Bob bought out Jim Betts' share of the Y.D.I. and is now associated with Ted in both enterprises. Bob is a member of S.N.A.M.E., N.A.M.S., S.S.C.D. and is a technical member of the A.B.Y.C. He is a frequent contributor of articles to the boating magazines, particularly Sail, and Motor Boating & Sailing.

Before moving to Maine to join Ted Brewer, Bob spent two years as a boatyard manager in Connecticut, a really valuable experience. As he says, "When you sit down at the drawing board to it's a great help to know how the things you are drawing up are actually put together by the shipwrights.

He is a qualified marine surveyor, and was invited to write a pamphlet entitled "Notes On Surveying In North America," which is used as a supplement to Ian Nicolson's book *Surveying Small Craft*.

Seeming to stand as an example of the adage that "the shoemaker's children never have shoes," Bob is a yacht designer without a boat at present. "We're so busy," he says, "there just doesn't seem to be time for it, but I sail on other people's boats whenever I can."

Preface

THE YACHT DESIGNER is made, not born, and there are a great many factors that go into his makeup. The ideas of the men under whom he works during the early stages of his career are a deciding influence. Almost equally so is the work of other designers, many he may never meet, whose creations he admires. Along with this go the hours of thinking and dreaming about future designs while spending long, dreary night watches at the helms of a variety of craft. And, as well, there are the boats themselves that he may have the fortune (or misfortune) to sail aboard which form part of his overall experience, and will certainly influence what he puts down on the drawing board. The sum of all these factors, along with the problems and successes of his previous designs, combine to give each designer a really individual approach to his work.

We trust this is reflected in our designs. While we do not specialize in any one type we hope that all of our work, whether a custom pinky schooner or a production fiberglass sloop, bears a stamp, however slight, that marks it for those who know. It's hard to define our philosophy but perhaps the major consideration is that a boat must be a pleasure to own. This means a craft that will do its intended work with a minimum of expense and fuss, provide its owner with dependable, sprightly performance and give him a solid return on his investment if he is ready to move on to bigger or better things.

If we can achieve all that we have done our job.

AN IMPORTANT NOTE ABOUT PLANS:

Please address all inquiries regarding plans shown in this book, or other Brewer & Wallstrom plans, to:
BREWER & ASSOCIATES
BROOKLIN, MAINE 04616

THE CRUISING AUXILIARY

Trends
In Hull Design

The past 50 years have seen more change (not necessarily "progress") in the design of yachts than there was in the preceding 200 years. Similarly, the last ten years have brought about more changes in basic hull design than did the 40 years before them. The strange thing about this continual process of evolution of ideas is that the sea and wind have remained the same for millions of years so we can only assume that we are right and all the seamen before us were wrong, or vice versa. Only the passage of time will decide whose judgment was correct.

In order to show the magnitude of the changes that have crept in during the last half century, we can set them down in tabular form. Of course, these are generalizations and there will always be exceptions to the rule but the table will give us a basic comparison.

In general, the above characteristics apply to craft of the ocean racing type. Inshore boats even in the '20s were apt to have longer overhangs and other "modern" features. As a rule the inshore racer or racer-cruiser has usually been ahead of its time in adopting new features since the consequences of rash or poor design are rarely as serious as in a long distance cruiser.

Still there have been exceptional yachts in every time period. Nat Herreshoff's *Gloriana*, built in 1890, was decades ahead of her time both in design and engineering. Her cutaway forefoot, wineglass midship section and fine keel set an example for others to follow for years to come. At the same time she presented such radically new ideas that she was condemned by all the "experts" and her features were not nearly as widely copied as they deserved to have been.

Despite the success of *Gloriana* and other brilliant designs the average cruiser and cruiser/racer of the '20s was more akin to the deep sea fishing boat than to the examples set by Herreshoff and others.

One reason that yachtsmen and designers ignored the few outstanding boats may be that seamen are very conservative traditionalists by

	1920s	1950s	1970s
Displ.	Heavy	Heavy-med.	Med.-light
Beam	Narrow	Wide	Wider
Overhangs	Short-med.	Long	Short
Bow O.H.	Short	Long	Med.-long
Stern O.H.	Long	Long	Short
Bow Entry	Full	Medium	Fine
Freeboard	Low	Medium	High
Keel Length	Long	Medium	Short
Ballast	Inside	Outside	Outside
Ball. Ratio	Low	Medium	High
Rig	Low & broad	Medium	High & nar.

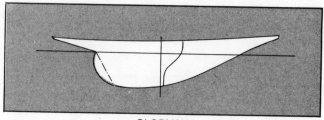

GLORIANA
The first modern keel boat.

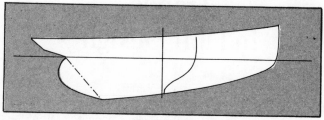

JOLIE BRISE
Winner of the 1925 Fastnet Race.
Built in 1919 as a pilot cutter.

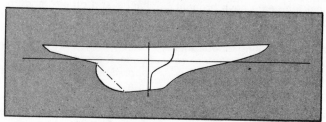

DRAGON CLASS SLOOP
An early light displacement
inshore racer.

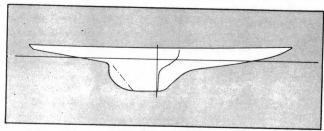

30 SQ. METER
Carrying a short keel and long
overhangs to the extreme.

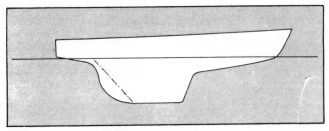

MYTH OF MALHAM
One of the first light displacement ocean racers.

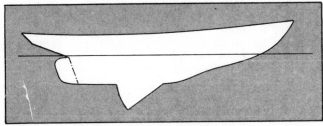

FINISTERRE
Successful and widely copied
keel-centerboard of the early '50s.

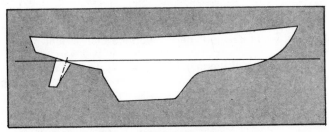

THE CAL 40
The start of a new breed.

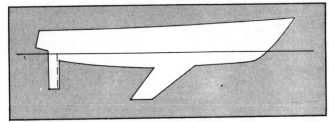

CHANCE 37
A modern fin keel ocean racer.

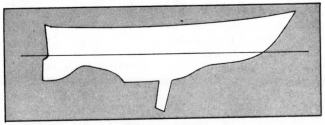

PEARSON 390
A modern keel-centerboard cruiser. Compare to *Finisterre.*

nature and reluctant to dispense with proven forms in favor of one new and relatively untried. D. Phillips-Birt has compared seamen to churchmen in their attitudes to change and observed that the cause may be that both deal in matters relatively difficult to prove.

A prime example of the conservatism of seamen is the staysail schooner *Nina* which won the Trans-Atlantic race in 1928. Today most of us would consider her to be a very heavy displacement, short ended cruising schooner if we were not aware of her winning ways. Yet when she was launched she was denounced as a dangerous rule beater by all the so-called experts. Indeed, such has been the lot of *Jullanar*, *America*, *Gloriana*, *Dorade*, Lapworth's Cal-40 and a number of other successful yachts, each of which, in one way or another, has advanced the knowledge of yacht design in her day.

Let us consider some of the major features in the design of a hull and discuss how the changes of 50 years have affected their seaworthiness and performance.

Displacement

The trend since 1920, indeed for many years before that, has been toward lighter and lighter displacement. We feel that this is a step in the right direction, provided that extremes of weak or overly costly construction are avoided, as boats (like steak or butter) are priced by the pound and the lighter vessel will cost less than a heavier yacht of similar size.

The light displacement hull must carry less sail area than the heavier boat since stability, or the power to carry sail, is a product of displacement times righting arm. However the light displacement hull does not require as much sail in order to obtain equal overall performance so the net result is a boat which is more easily handled and maintained.

As well, with the advent of aluminum and fiberglass, we are seeing light displacement boats built with ballast ratios much higher than were achieved on the normal cruiser-racer of the past. This lowers the center of gravity of course and so lengthens the righting arm with the result that we now have light displacement craft of a stability comparable to older medium-heavy displacement hulls. These newer yachts thus have the power to carry sufficient sail to perform exceptionally well in all conditions.

In the realm of performance, most yachtsmen believe that the heavy boat will be superior in rough going. This is not the case necessarily as a check of race results of the past years would show. In pure boat for boat speed the heavy hull often shows best in light weather since she will have little, if any, more wetted surface than a light hull of the same size and will normally be carrying a great deal more sail.

In the lower speed-length ratios the major part of resistance derives from surface friction so that the very much higher sail area/wetted surface ratios of the heavy displacement hull will prove to be a deciding factor in a light weather race.

In heavier breezes, where boat speeds are relatively high, the amount of resistance depends largely upon wave making and this is a product of the speed and displacement of the hull. The length of the wave is increased by an increase in hull speed and the size, or depth, of the wave is governed by the displacement of the hull; the more displacement the larger the wave.

Wave making resistance is the energy lost in forming these waves so it is obvious that the heavy displacement hull will divert more of its sail power to wave making than will its lighter sister and will actually be at a disadvantage in heavy weather sailing.

The result is that the light displacement hull can achieve the same performance in heavy weather with less sail and so be easier to handle. Similarly, when ballasted sufficiently to enable it to carry almost as much sail as the heavy displacement hull, the lighter boat can be faster.

Overhangs

The motion of a light displacement hull in a sea is somewhat quicker than that of her heavier sister, true, but the motion is not nearly as quick or uncomfortable as proponents of the heavy displacement hull would have us believe. Early light displacement craft were inshore racers of the Dragon, 22 and 30 square meter and similar types with short waterlines and long overhangs. These yachts had a quick motion as a result of the lifting action of the seas on their long buoyant ends and earned a reputation that has clung to light displacement hulls ever since.

Modern hulls with their fairly short ends are comparatively comfortable in all weathers, quite dry on deck and easy to move about on.

We feel that the length of overhang should be related to the displacement and in our opinion it is the heavy displacement hulls that require long overhangs in order to provide sufficient reserve buoyancy in heavy seas to lift the weight of the hull and assure dryness on deck.

Possibly the poorest hull forms in regard to design of the ends were some of the turn of the century yachts and workboats with plumb bows and long overhanging counters. Such a boat would be prone to dipping its nose like a submarine into every large sea due to lack of reserve buoyancy forward. Anyone working on the bowsprit received a thorough drenching while, at the same time, the long counter was lifting the aft end so that the vessel was in danger of tripping with a resultant broach.

The modern yacht with moderate bow overhang and short stern over-

hang is exactly the opposite of most of the older craft. The bow provides buoyancy enabling the vessel to ride up and over the seas instead of driving through them. This results in less resistance as well as a dry deck while the short stern prevents the aft end from being lifted excessively. This reduces the danger of tripping to some extent and eliminates the hobby horsing to which many long ended light displacement craft of the past were prone.

A further advantage of the modern short ends is that they produce yachts with the long waterline necessary for higher potential speeds.

Freeboard

One problem of the early light displacement hulls was lack of accommodations. Tumlarens, Dragons, square meter boats and other light inshore racers of the past were fortunate if they had two berths, sitting headroom and a stove shelf in a 28-30' hull.

Part of the reason for this was the yachtsman's prejudice against high freeboard. This was based partly on the desire for "traditional" appearance and partly on the fact that many cruising boats of the '20s were miniatures of sailing workboats where low freeboard was a necessity for the hauling of nets. Since such working craft had to be at sea in all weathers, their features were imitated in the belief that they denoted seaworthiness.

While hulls were of very heavy displacement, low freeboard was acceptable due to the space available within the hull for accommodations. The move to higher freeboard in order to obtain reasonable accommodations in a light displacement hull received impetus from Laurent Giles' very successful *Myth of Malham* and similar boats in the late '40s. As well, the Cruising Club of America handicap rule at that time gave a bonus for high freeboard up to a point so that the yachtsman of the '50s was becoming accustomed to seeing higher and higher freeboard and learning to accept the benefits that accompanied it.

Still it was not until fiberglass production methods brought the cost of yachting within reach of a wider group of enthusiasts (and Lapworth brought out his Cal 40) that the lighter hull types jumped in popularity. With this jump came the demand for family cruising accommodations that could only be satisfied by higher freeboard, along with greater beam.

One need only look at the cruisers of the '30s and '40s to see how many changes have been made in the interior accommodation. Even in the heavy displacement hulls of those days it was generally conceded that no yacht under 30 feet could have standing headroom and that one had to go over 30' to work in four berths. Now we see five and six berths combined with full headroom in a 26 or 27 footer!

Of course, accommodations are not everything but the trend to higher freeboard has also given us greater reserve stability along with drier decks, thus making the vessel a better working platform. We do obtain added windage and a higher center of gravity, obviously. However, this has been much more than offset by the high ballast ratios achieved by modern construction techniques and materials so that a stiffer hull results despite the minor drawbacks of high freeboard.

Beam

Another benefit of the CCA rule of the '50s was that it encouraged the beamy keel centerboard yacht such as Olin Stephens' famous *Finisterre*. This started a trend toward greater beam that continues to this day in yachts of all types, both deep keel and keel centerboard.

The advantage of added interior space is apparent but beam also increases the length of the righting arm. As stated earlier, stability is a product of displacement times righting arm so that a beamy light displacement hull can have generally the same sail carrying power as her narrow, heavy displacement sister. When the generous beam is coupled with high freeboard, the modern cruiser may well have more stability over a longer range than her older counterpart.

Of course, like many another good thing, beam can be carried too far. An increase in beam generates an increase in resistance which is more than compensated for normally by the added sail permitted by the greater stability of the reduced heel angle which improves the efficiency of the rig and the keel. However, excess beam may lead to poor steering characteristics or to an unacceptable increase in resistance, particularly in short, choppy seas when sailing on the wind.

Other drawbacks of excess beam are a snappier motion and an increase in wetted surface, both more or less cancelled out by the added sail area that can be carried.

Unfortunately no line can be drawn between "generous" and "excess" beam and it is one of the fine points of yacht design that must be left to the judgment of the architect and, perhaps, the test tank. However, since catboats commonly sail well with beams approaching half of their overall length it might be said that we are still a long way from reaching the ultimate on the average cruiser. Certainly the benefits of wide beam to a light displacement hull more than outweigh its minor disadvantages at this point.

Keel Length

Although fin keels were popular at the turn of the century they were not commonly used for offshore yachts until the mid '60s. Offshore cruisers and racers had long keels with raking rudder posts and deep forefeet, akin to those on the commercial fishing boats, in the belief that this was the most seaworthy type possible. What many yachtsmen of the time overlooked was that the workboats spent as much time hove to as they did sailing and the lateral plane was designed with that in mind.

At the same time the keels on inshore racing yachts were getting progressively shorter throughout the years but the rudders were hung on the aft end of the keel with few exceptions. This worked reasonably well on the long, narrow hulls such as the square meter types, as the hulls themselves provided considerable course keeping ability. However, the use of a super short fin with keel hung rudder was not always a happy combination on a beamy hull.

Laurent Giles was designing fin keel/spade rudder boats for offshore use in the early '50s, *Sopranino*, *Trekka* (the smallest yacht to circumnavigate the world, 20'10" LOA), and *Gypsella* are a few examples of his pioneering in light displacement types with fin keels and separate rudders. There were pioneers on this side of the Atlantic as well but it was not until the success of the Cal 40 that the short fin keel with spade or skeg hung rudder really came into its own.

The advantages of the fin for racing are obvious. Wetted surface is reduced, aspect ratio increased and performance improved as a result. The rudder mounted well aft contributes to good steering due to its greater leverage. However, we feel that for the pure cruising boat the trend to short fin keels and separate rudders has been rather overdone. The combination can work well of couse. Indeed Illingworth reported that *Myth of Malham* was capable of being left to herself for reasonable periods of time and she had a very short fin with the rudder mounted on it well forward of the aft end of the waterline. Still, for cruising, we feel the fin should be of reasonable length and the rudder of generous size fitted well aft on a large skeg if it is to provide a comfortably steady helm. A full keel of moderate length will be preferred by many, of course, and it has the advantage that draft can be reduced compared to a fin with no great increase in luxury.

The modern trend appears to be to design boats for two specific purposes, racing and cruising. It is probable that we will see a greater division in types in future years each with their distinctive lateral plane. The racers will tend to even more extreme fins while the cruisers will continue to lean towards longer fins or full keels. However, a change in the handicap rules, taking actual lateral plane area or fin aspect ratio into account, could alter this drastically and even things out again.

Cost

The cost of a light displacement hull can be high on a per pound basis if extravagant forms of construction are used. In the past years when wood was the prime component of yachts, it required very skilled and expensive workmanship in a high quality yard to turn out a good light displacement hull.

The modern fiberglass production hull on the other hand does not require such costly and hard to acquire skills so light displacement hulls can be ground out of a mold for the same cost as a heavy displacement hull. Since the hull is only a small percentage of the overall cost of the boat and the light displacement craft requires less ballast, lighter spars and rigging, less sail area, smaller engine and lighter hardware than its heavier sister the total cost of such a vessel is substantially less than that of a heavy displacement craft of the same general size.

In general, we feel that the design trends of the last 50 years have been healthy ones. There have always been extremes in design, there always will be, but the average modern cruiser and cruiser-racer is a good craft for its purpose, costing less and generally performing better than its predecessors under all conditions.

13

Performance
and The Cruising Boat

I lost track, long ago, of the number of times I have heard the following request, "We need a design for a xx foot auxiliary. It must be seaworthy as we plan extensive voyages but we do not require really good performance for we don't intend to do any racing."

These yachtsmen, like many others, equate seaworthiness and comfort with a slow vessel. In fact the ideal for such owners can be seen in the Tahiti ketch — extremely heavy displacement for her size, a long keel, deep forefoot, double ended hull and gaff ketch rig, very short on area (for ease of handling, of course).

There is no doubt that such boats are capable of long, offshore voyages and can endure severe weather conditions. Yet lighter, handier yachts with better performance all round have shown time and again that they can do the same. In my opinion the typical husky double ended ketch has numerous faults and I will review a few of the major ones.

As a rule, such craft are far too heavily built and this adds enormously to the cost of materials and labor. Generally, such designs ignore modern construction materials or techniques and depend on massive framing, knees and bolts to achieve what is better done by bronze barb nails and glue or, alternately, ferrocement, fiberglass or welded metal. As a result of heavy construction, the displacement ratio is very low. The first increases resistance, the second decreases stability and both result in poor performance.

My complaint against super heavy displacement goes beyond its effect on performance. Let's consider two boats, the first a 30 foot "husky" auxiliary of 20,000 lbs. displacement and the second a similar size craft of 10,000 lbs. displacement. If both vessels have the same general freeboard and hull volume above water, obviously they will have the same reserve buoyancy. When the light boat runs into heavy seas, this reserve buoyancy will be sufficient to lift its 10,000 lbs. of weight, albeit with a relatively quick motion, resulting in a dry and comfortable craft. The heavy hull may have an easier motion but in a heavy sea its decks will be swept like a half tide rock. This is not conducive either to comfort or seaworthiness!

In a gale with a rocky coast to leeward, the cruising man needs a boat that can point high under reefed sail, tack quickly and positively and get him out of there in one piece. What he doesn't need is a boat that can barely tack through 110-120° and loses thirty yards of precious sea room every time she comes about; yet this is exactly the type of boat many dream about when they say, "I don't require performance as I won't be doing any racing."

In the lighter breezes common to many of our coasts, the "husky" cruising boat may not come about at all and will find itself in irons time and again. When it does come about after backing the jib and/or turning on the engine, it sails off on the other tack with all the speed and grace of a can buoy. As a result, if you look around most of our marinas you will find many of these vessels tied to the docks ("not enough breeze") while owners of better performing craft are out enjoying themselves.

The gaff ketch rig beloved by many dyed-in-the-wool cruising men adds to the problem as it is about the worst rig possible to put on a hull that already has two strikes against it. In fact the 1955 RORC rule equated the efficiency of the various rigs as follows:

Bermudan sloop or cutter	100%
Bermudan yawl	96%
Bermudan schooner, gaff	
sloop or cutter	92%
Bermudan ketch, gaff yawl	88%
Gaff schooner	85%
Gaff ketch	81%

Obviously, when you tie a gaff rig onto a heavy, long keeled, lightly ballasted hull you cannot expect sparkling performance to be the result. Douglas Phillips-Birt, writing about motorsailers, suggested that heavy, full bodied craft with inefficient lateral plane needed an efficient rig of reasonably high aspect ratio in order to obtain good windward performance.

The same thinking might well apply to the pure cruising boat. Certainly a gaff ketch rig hardly merits the description of an efficient, high aspect ratio sail plan yet this is the rig that may be called on to pull a beamy, full bodied hull to windward in an emergency.

Other faults of many "husky" cruisers are those already described in my previous articles; overly full waterlines forward, too short a run aft, unnecessarily shoal draft, poorly shaped rudders, etc., all of which detract from the decent performance that may be necessary for safety on that one dire occasion.

This is not to say the ultimate ocean racing machine is a perfect cruiser because of its superior windward ability; nor that a converted 6-,

8- or 12-meter yacht is going to satisfy the needs of the cruising yachtsman. Such vessels usually lack the amenities desired for comfortable living aboard and, as well, may be built to lesser standards of durability than a good cruiser. Again this has to be qualified by saying that a light but superbly built meter boat of bronze fastened mahogany and other top materials is going to be stronger and more maintenance-free than a poorly built iron fastened spruce planked tub regardless of how heavy the scantlings. However, there *is* a happy medium between the two extremes and this is where a well designed cruiser should fit in.

So what is the perfect cruising boat? There is no perfect boat, of course, due to the varying requirements of each individual owner. However, I will stick my neck out on a limb just a bit and lay down a few criteria.

First, it must be light, strong, durable and have low maintenance. For a custom boat in order of preference, and considering initial cost, I would select laminated mahogany (perhaps polypropylene covered), strip planked, double planked, steel, ferro-cement, fiberglass and welded aluminum in about that order. If cost were no object, the aluminum hull would be much higher on the list as would the one-off fiberglass.

Please note I have not included single carvel planking as I feel other methods are superior. However, when the price is very right, as from many foreign yards, a well built single planked carvel boat is certainly acceptable. By now, you may have ascertained that "well built" when applied to a wooden hull means bronze, copper, mahogany, teak and white oak. It does *not* mean red oak, birch, galvanized nails, black spruce, etc.

Since the major cost of any craft today is in labor, it can cost almost as much to assemble third rate materials as it does to assemble first rate. The difference in material costs is insignificant in comparison, particularly when maintenance costs and resale value are considered.

The perfect cruiser should also have a hull form that is easily steered, reasonably steady on the helm, stable, comfortable and weatherly. To my mind this means a keel of medium length, not a pure fin, not a typical workboat keel (after all, working fishing boats were designed to heave to for fishing, not to sail well).

L. Francis Herreshoff has designed some very beautiful craft with underwater profiles that seem to be perfect for cruising — ample length of keel for steadiness on the helm but incorporating a well cut away forefoot and a cut away sternpost and rudder. It is perhaps the perfect combination for all round cruising with the advantage that the rudder is unlikely to be damaged if a forgetful hand (it's never the skipper's fault!)

does put her on the bricks.

In recent months several experienced owners have specified new designs with 6 foot draft. In a larger vessel, say over 35' waterline, this may mean going to a centerboard hull form, yet it has the advantage that the boat can be taken anywhere in the world outside the one fathom line on the charts with reasonable assurance.

In a smaller offshore cruiser, going to the 5'6" to 6'0" draft range may be advisable in that the same one fathom line restriction would apply, yet the smaller the boat, the more is to be gained in windward ability and stability from the maximum reasonable draft. The owner who specifies 4' or 4½' draft in a long distance cruiser may not be realistically appraising her future cruising needs or navigational requirements.

Displacement should be moderate,

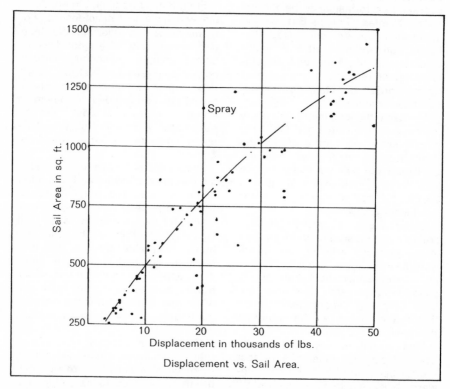

Displacement vs. Sail Area.

neither too heavy nor too light. The heavy hull has the faults previously mentioned while a too light displacement restricts the amount of stores and gear that may be carried without overloading. Unfortunately there is no neat table that can be set down giving a suitable displacement for any given size. The accompanying charts showing displacement related to LWL, and sail area related to displacement were plotted from information in the *Sailboat and Sailboat Equipment Directory*, Baader's *The Sailing Yacht*, *Yachting's Book of .Plans* plus my own rather extensive crib files. The plots are a cross-section of all types of vessels by leading designers. It can be seen that the *Spray* (data from *Baader*) was neither heavy displacement for her length nor undercanvassed.

As for rig, I would select a Bermudan cutter, yawl or ketch in that order. A cutter is very weatherly, not difficult to handle and the midship mast location permits a strongly stayed rig. A yawl, if the mizzen is of more than handkerchief size, can be a handy rig as well, more weatherly than the ketch and yet able to jog along under jib and mizzen if that mast is strongly designed and stayed.

The Bermudan ketch is easy to handle and though not as weatherly as the yawl it can be balanced under a wider variety of reduced sail combinations as a rule. Of course, rig choice depends on size to a large extent but cutters up to 40' or so are practical even with a small crew. And a gaff cutter is still a reasonably efficient rig for those whose love for the gaff rig remains immune to persuasion.

Regardless of the rig selected it should be of ample area for light weather yet easily shortened down for heavy going. Bear in mind that,

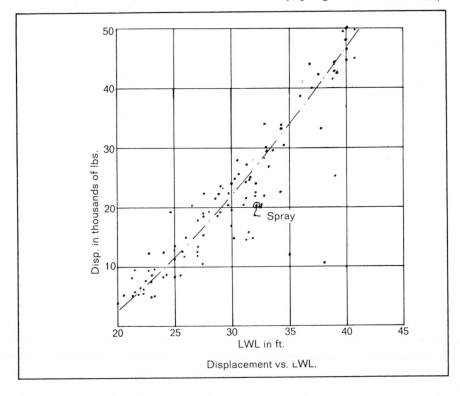

Displacement vs. LWL.

where racing handicap rules do not apply, it is easier to shorten sail by reefing than it is to increase it by use of genoa jibs, reachers, spinnakers and other light weather sails.

Modern roller reefing and roller furling gears make sail area adjustment relatively simple and fast for the cruising man. The long distance offshore cruiser might also investigate the use of self-steering twin headsails for their advantages of simplicity in downwind sailing.

Sail lacings, cotton sails, manila halyards and the like have no more place on a modern distance cruiser than square sails, deadeyes and treenails, in my opinion. They are all fun on coastal cruising character boats where a safe port is always handy. And we all know they have weathered many a storm. But I would no more go back to them on a boat on which my life depended than I would revert to two wheel brakes, cone clutch, carbide lamps and friction shock absorbers on my car.

Modern technology has left them behind and nostalgia, sweet as it may be, is not common sense when your life is at stake, as it well could be in a cruising yacht under extreme conditions. The tremendous strains of ocean racing have forced the development of modern gear that is as strong, dependable and more efficient than anything the old timers used. Of course, there is a lot of junk available too, but that is true whether you are buying a mast hoop or stainless steel sail track.

Another feature I don't like to see on an offshore cruiser is a mast stepped on deck. It is acceptable if it is mounted in a solid tabernacle but a mast stepped in a cup on the cabin roof has several weaknesses. It is only half as strong in compression for a given section as when it is stepped down on the keel and well supported at the deck. Also, if it does go over the side it usually goes all the way while a keel stepped mast may leave enough of a stub remaining to permit a jury rig to be set up. I definitely feel it is safer.

To summarize, regardless of the arrangement, or construction, a comfortable long distance cruiser should be an able, weatherly vessel with good all around performance in light breezes or strong winds. Such performance is the result of the proper combination of hull, rig and sail area. It does not come from a mismatched and inefficient, short area sail plan propelling a bulky, stubby hull, nor does it come from a towering super high aspect ratio rig on a super light, skimming dish. There *is* a happy medium!

Selecting A Design

The first step in turning the dream of building your own boat into a reality is the selection of the right design. The amateur builder is looking for a boat that is within his financial reach, of course, and also within his ability to construct to reasonable standards. Moreover, he wants a design that satisfies his requirements as to size, type, rig and accommodations.

Unfortunately, the average amateur builder is often not sufficiently knowledgeable to select a plan that meets these needs and is, at the same time, a technically correct design. Too many would-be builders are attracted by a spacious and comfortable accommodation arrangement without giving sufficient thought to the hull shape that is going to carry that interior or the rig that is going to propel it. They trust that the designer has done his job properly.

Some available plans are not only designs of unattractive, poor-performing craft but also of possibly dangerously unseaworthy boats as well.

A prospective amateur builder showed me a brochure on a cruising boat in the mid-40-foot range and requested that I comment on the merits of the vessel. The builder of this boat could have been in serious trouble without some sound advice.

The boat featured in the brochure may have been an outstanding example of innocence and ignorance on the part of a so-called "yacht designer," but I fear that it was just one of a number of such plans that are being pushed at amateur builders. Briefly a few of the faults of the design were as follows:

—boat was of excessively heavy displacement (displacement-length ratio of 455), very small sail area (sail area-displacement ratio of 10.5), and of unusually low ballast-displacement ratio (18.5%). Its performance at best would be disappointing and at worst, hazardous, hardly satisfactory for what the brochure described as a "seagoing auxiliary."

—the mainmast was stepped directly on the keel with no mast step to spread the load, a dangerously weak construction inviting serious future problems.

—the propeller shaft was over 12' long with no sign of an intermediate bearing. This would probably lead to major problems of shaft whipping.

—the lateral plane was a rather curious shape, the keel being deepest at its forward end and shoalest at the rudder post. This configuration is typical of Arabian dhows, but Fenger was the only modern designer to use such a shape as he felt it worked well with his "Fenger" rig. The design in question was not Fenger rigged. My feeling is that the unusual lateral plane would pose sail balance problems and possibly poor steering under quartering wind and sea conditions.

—the mooring cleats intended to hold a 25-ton boat were only of 8" size, not really adequate for a yacht of half that displacement.

—the winches for a rig of almost 1100 sq. ft. consisted of only two

Merriman #3's for the jib sheets, about what one would see today on a 25 footer. There were no indications of a mainsheet winch, a staysail sheet winch, or any cleats for these sails.

—the bow pulpit was formed of "half inch diameter stainless steel or brass tubing," not even remotely adequate for a 20′ trailer cruiser, much less a boat over twice that length.

—the deck layout showed no genoa tracks, jib sheet pad-eyes, cleats, staysail sheet fairleads or other useful hardware normally fitted to a sailboat.

—ventilation consisted of only two small dorade vents for three cabins plus heads. There was no sign of engine room ventilators.

The above faults were evident on a cursory examination of the brochure. A thorough review of the complete set of plans would undoubtedly reveal a great many more.

In short, this boat appeared to have been designed by someone without the slightest experience of sailing or sailing yacht design, yet it was offered as a sea-going vessel suitable for amateur construction. Surprisingly, it was not offered by some unknown young designer but by a supposedly reputable firm. It is interesting to note, though, that the brochure did not give the name of the "expert" who drew up this dream ship.

The ethics of a firm that would try to sell a design of such poor quality to amateur builders is open to serious question. I am angry to discover that my profession contains such men.

Of more immediate interest, however, is a method by which amateur builders can identify and avoid the purchase of similar plans.

The first step is to familiarize yourself with the proportions and details of sound, well designed boats so that you can spot the few that are obviously incompetently designed. A study of the design sections of the boating magazines and directories can supply a wealth of information on average displacements, LOA/LWL ratios, beam/waterline ratios, draft, ballast ratios, sail area, rig proportions, power plants, and other details.

Clip out the designs of particular interest and start a "crib" file so that you have a basis for serious comparison when you consider plans for your own boat.

Next, obtain some good books on yacht design and read them thoroughly with emphasis on the sections dealing with proportion, construction, and details of deck layouts, rigs, machinery, etc. In particular, I recommend *Sailing Yachts* by Juan Baader, *Elements of Yacht Design* by Francis Kinney, *Sailing Yacht Design* by Douglas Phillips-Birt, *Offshore* by John Illingworth or any of Eric Hiscock's fine books.

For information on wood construction study *Boatbuilding* by Howard Chapelle or Robert Steward's *Manual of Boatbuilding;* for ferrocement, Jay Benford's *Practical Ferrocement Boatbuilding.* Unfortunately, there are few good books on fiberglass other than those of a very technical nature, but Bruce Roberts' *Amateur Fiberglass Boatbuilding* contains worthwhile information for the amateur builder.

There are many other books available covering various aspects of design and construction and the ones mentioned above are just a sampling. I realize that working your way through such a pile of reading matter is a tedious step for someone anxious to start building his own boat, but a month of study could well save several years of wasted labor along with thousands of dollars worth of material.

Finally, visit all the boat yards in your area and again study closely the type of yacht which you intend to build. Look carefully at hardware, deck layouts, rigging and, if it is off season, underwater shapes and proportions. While giving these craft a thorough going over, it is a good idea to have a notebook and camera in hand to record particularly interesting details and ideas which you can incorporate in your own boat while under construction. Few designs are so good that they cannot be improved upon.

While you acquire knowledge of yacht design, you probably will already have begun collecting brochures on plans of the type of craft that interest you. First, discard any that do not bear the designer's name.

It is evident from the brochure I saw that at least one firm is using inexperienced draftsmen to draw up plans and then is selling these plans as "company" designs without checking on the quality of the work. A legitimate naval architect would not allow a firm to sell his designs without insisting that he be acknowledged as the designer. If you cannot ascertain the architect's name, you have no way of looking into his technical ability, his reputation or his experience.

The second step is to study the details of the designs to the degree that the small scale drawings in the brochures permit. Check the adequacy of deck hardware, such as cleats, winches, sheet fittings, ventilation, etc. If you find a number of minor details that are obviously poor, the chances are good that some of the major points in the plans will also be wrong although they may not be so obvious to an amateur builder. Here your crib files will be useful.

You can be reasonably certain that the work of leading designers such as Olin Stephens, George Cuthbertson, Dick Carter, Alan Gurney, Gary Mull, John Atkin, and McCurdy & Rhodes is technically correct. If the plans you are considering do not match their work in accuracy of detail, proportions, styling (according to type) and other particulars, take a second, closer look at them and discard those that do not match up to rea-

sonable standards.

On the other hand, do not shy from an otherwise suitable set of plans simply because the designer is relatively unknown. There will always be a new crop of promising young architects trying to get a start and many of these have both the talent and knowledge to design an excellent yacht.

Do not hesitate to write the designer to ask about his qualifications, experience and previously successfully designed craft. A reasonably long apprenticeship with a well-known yacht designer or design firm is an excellent recommendation as is membership in the Society of Naval Architects and Marine Engineers or the Society of Small Craft Designers. However, such societies have "student" and "associate" members who may or may not be as well qualified in yacht design as a designer with the status of a full member. Even graduation from a recognized school of yacht design, whether by correspondence or at the university level, is not necessarily a sign of competence since it does not guarantee that the designer has the necessary practical background.

At Yacht Design Institute we recommend that our students work for a successful designer for several years before setting up their own office. We feel this is the best possible way to obtain the practical experience necessary to meet the needs of future clients. The capable architect will also have considerable sailing time aboard both his own designs and other vessels, but this is a qualification that can be difficult to check.

Obviously, the finest recommendation for a designer's work is a successful boat already built to the plans in which you are interested. However, many successful designers do not like to release client's names and addresses since it can be an imposition upon the owner to be asked to show his boat or to have to answer long inquiries. Of course, it does not hurt to try to see the boat or write the owner, particularly if you are doubtful about the suitability of the design for your needs.

If you are very much interested in the design, the architect may sell study plans at a fraction of the cost of the full set of drawings. As a rule, the cost of the study plans is applicable against the design fee, so you lose nothing if you go ahead at a later date.

The study plans normally include a large scale sail plan, arrangement plan, inboard profile and some construction drawings, possibly a construction section and/or profile. These plans should let you determine whether the designer knows his business. If there is still any doubt, consult with a more experienced amateur builder, a professional builder, or another designer. However, be prepared to pay a consultation fee when you seek professional advice, although it will be well worth the cost if such advice saves you from an expensive mistake.

In summary, the best way to avoid a dud design is to increase your own expertise to the point where you can recognize incompetence when you see it. Then, if in doubt, obtain professional advice. Nothing could be more to the point than the adage "look before you leap." A blind leap into building a poorly designed craft will give you more agony, expense and frustration than any man needs in one lifetime, yet it is a simple matter to avoid such problems if you plan ahead.

(Ted Brewer does not make a practice of commenting on designs sent to him by readers although he is available for professional consultation. — Ed.)

Layout...
and Performance

Can a boat's interior arrangement affect performance? If you have been following this series, you will know it can. Interior joinerwork is weight and any weight added to the hull means less ballast can be carried on a given displacement. This means less stability which in turn means less power to carry sail, and this translates finally into reduced performance.

We have already discussed the fact that getting the weight out of the ends decreases pitching which means better windward ability.

A study of some of the ocean racing designs reviewed in the "Keelbolts and Sailplans" column in recent months shows that the high performance designers are concentrating the living arrangements amidships and using the forepeak for sail stowage.

In fact, in his "Designer's Comments" for *Improbable*, Gary Mull emphasized that all major weights were designed for an area around midships and that an attempt was made to keep them in a section about 30% of boat length to ensure that they were well concentrated.

A wise owner will take a tip from this and reduce weight aloft, below, and in the ends. Heavy anchors, chain or tanks in the forepeak are not conducive to good windward performance.

With some work it is usually possible to move many of these items aft and store them low in the bilges amidships when racing. Much of the gear that can accumulate in the ends may even be better if left ashore; particularly half empty cans of paint and varnish, or the old rusted tools beloved by so many owners.

Of course, if major weights are moved, it may affect trim or stability and mean that remeasuring is necessary. The owner who foresees such an eventuality should check with his measurer.

A study of the "hot" designs will also reveal that the out-and-out ocean racers are cutting way back on luxuries and frills in order to keep these weights as light as possible. Racing layouts are tending to fewer berths, smaller galleys and less complete facilities throughout.

If you think about it, it does make sense. The go-go ocean racing crew has no objection to sleeping *hot bunk* if it makes the boat a mite faster, so there is really no need to have a private berth for every man aboard.

The skipper/navigator and the cook should have their own berths, of course, as they stand regular watch and their duties keep them up and down at all hours. However, the winch grinders, sheet tweakers and wheel twirlers can use the hot bunk method without problem.

But if you look at the arrangement plan of almost any stock boat you find it is crammed with more berths than will ever be necessary (unless the owner is a masochist!). It is not unusual to see five or six berths on a 26 footer, eight on a 35 footer and nine or more on a 40 footer!

It seems the number of berths

crowded into one undersize boat is getting to be a measure of a designer's skill! Yet have you ever cruised for two weeks on a 26 footer with four other people?

It is inhuman torture at best and if any of the other four are children it can lead to insanity. As one humorist put it, he knew some children who could make the *Queen Mary* seem like a crowded rowboat!

Unfortunately, smaller boats are more apt to have excess sleeping accommodations than larger craft, perhaps because their owners are more likely to be novices and include this large sleeping capacity in their measurements of quality.

These same boats rarely have sufficient storage areas for sails, life jackets, inflatable dinghies or other gear. The result is that the equipment winds up on the forward V berths, which would have been better designed as sail bins in the first place.

Beyond the fact that forward berths put the weight of the off-watch too far forward and limit storage space for light sails, they are not the best place to obtain a good rest when the boat is pounding into a head sea.

Under such conditions it is not unusual to see a man drag his sleeping bag aft into the saloon, where the motion is less severe, and curl up on the cabin sole for 40 winks. I've done it myself.

If family circumstances make forward V berths essential, it is better to have sail bins *under* them rather than just a few tiny drawers and lockers. This can be done either by having the whole berth bottom hinged as on *Amee*, a recent 37 foot design of ours (see figure 1), or by building actual sail bins and fitting a pipe cot over them.

Two big advantages of pipe cots are lightness and comfort. An aluminum frame with a laced in dacron bottom and a 1″-2″ foam mattress is equally or more comfortable than a solid plywood berth bottom with a 4″ foam mattress; and it weighs about half as much. It can be hinged up or down to compensate for heel and this is a great comfort on a long haul.

Dacron-bottom berths are feasible for any berth that doesn't have to do double duty as a seat, and the overall weight saving can be very substantial. Perhaps the epitome of lightness in berths were the dacron bottomed ones we fitted to *American Eagle* for the America's Cup trials. They were foam mattresses only ¼″ thick (the rules insisted on a mattress for each berth!) yet they were quite comfortable.

In my opinion, one of the abominations of the modern stock boat is the convertible dinette. At sea it is almost impossible to sit facing fore and aft and as a result, many boats I have raced aboard with this layout have left the table ashore and used the "dinette" as a regular single settee-berth.

A settee-berth port and starboard, with a permanent pilot berth outboard (where beam permits) is a more comfortable and convivial arrangement. Even an upper/lower berth arrangement is better at sea, for the uppers can be dacron bottom pipe frames and can be adjusted for heel angle.

The dinette is useful in port of course, but so is a standard layout with a strong folding table. Speaking of tables, I am not fond of the gimballed type. They are very heavy and while it is true the food stays put, the windward eaters are doubled over to eat with the table at shin level, and the leeward diners are reaching up with their grub at eye height.

It takes a beamy and stiff hull that sails on her bottom to use a gimballed table to advantage. And even then if you've ever had a 50 pound table thump down on your kneecap while you're having lunch you will think twice about the blessings of gimbals!

Figure 1

Amee, a recent design by Ted Brewer.

Other places to save weight are heavy locker doors and drawers that many craft are fitted with. The handicap rules do not make an allowance for the weight of joinerwork and it becomes more difficult every year for an average older craft to compete with the newer stripped out custom machines.

An owner trying to keep an older yacht competitive might look at his joinerwork to see if some of it can be replaced with lighter plywood (or even dacron) locker fronts, doors, etc.

Perhaps the epitome of the stripped out inshore racer was Bill Luders' 39' sloop *Storm.* Her galley consisted of a one burner gimballed sterno

stove and a basin that had to be lifted out and emptied over the side.

There were no hanging locker, ice box, drawers, etc.; just two pipe berths, two settee berths and a toilet in a rather exposed location. When the boat was racing, tinned goods and other foods were usually laid out neatly on the cabin sole. One had to crawl over them to move around, and as she had only sitting headroom this was not always easy.

Storm was not what anyone would call a comfortable cruiser but she won more than her share of races, and it was fun to sail aboard her for that reason.

While such a yacht is fine for an overnight race, or even a three-day

Construction is of strip planked white pine on bulkhead framing, fiberglass covered. Unusual features are her twin tabs and the winch handle on the binnacle that cross connects with both of the Barient 30's.

She has many ingenious mechanical devices invented by her owner, including a folding spinnaker pole and a saloon table which raises and lowers by a winch. The V berths have sail bins under them.

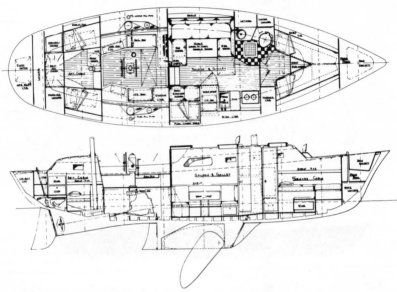

race with a young and eager crew, she leaves much to be desired for a longer haul, primarily due to her inability to provide good meals.

The galley is one place I like to see well equipped. Weight is not so important here for the galley is usually located close to the center of buoyancy. I'm a hearty eater at sea myself and I believe a well fed crew is a happy and efficient crew. Pork and beans and peanut butter sandwiches are fine in their place but a steady diet of them soon palls.

A good galley is one where the cook can turn out food that will brighten a tired man's day and put heart into an oncoming watch. For this reason I favor a gimballed stove with an oven and electric or mechanical refrigeration for a long race or voyage. They both help the cook do his job properly.

A deep freeze is a great asset if a boat is going to be at sea for a week or more, for good solid meals can be cooked ashore and kept until needed, then quickly reheated. Boats 40' or under can be fitted with refrigeration and deep freeze by use of engine driven pumps and holding plates.

On boats without such refrigeration units the cook might consider pre-packaged dehydrated and freeze dried foods that are now widely available. Freeze dried meats are not the same as a roast of beef but they are a long way ahead of pork and beans or tinned stew. And they are easily prepared.

A rested, well-fed crew will help any boat reach its potential on a long haul. If you can make your crew content, lighten the ship and get the weight out of her ends, you will have done a great deal toward increasing your boat's sailing performance.

The cruising man's problems are a bit different from those of the cruiser-racer for performance here takes second place to comfort and convenience.

However, forward V berths are still not the best spot for sleeping at sea and convertible dinettes are not the ideal seating space for a 20° angle of heel unless the cushions and the seat of your pants are fitted with velcro tape.

If you find you are not using the V berths and that they are always piled with sails, the space might be better utilized as a combined work bench/sail bin area. I am not suggesting that you tear out a dinette, but if you are buying a new boat and have a choice between a dinette and a settee/pilot berth arrangement, I recommend the latter.

Remember that some stock boat builders are not out to give the buyer what he needs, or wants, but rather what Madison Avenue *thinks* he wants. Remember too that you won't be using that dinette as the boat stands on the showroom floor but at 20-30° angle of heel heading into a head sea.

One *last* word on dinettes, if you must have one, a U shaped type will be more comfortable than the straight athwartship one for a large part of the seating area runs fore and aft and is reasonably usable at sea.

Obtaining Proper Balance

Balance is the quality that makes a boat easily and lightly steered, under even severe conditions, without either lee helm or excess weather helm. As we have mentioned in previous articles, some weather helm is desirable so that rudder area will contribute to lift, and aid in counteracting leeway. A weather helm of 2-4° is said to produce the best windward ability and give the helmsman a solid feel of the boat.

To achieve proper balance, a designer lays out his sailplan so that the center of effort (CE) of the sails is the proper distance ahead of the center of lateral plane (CLP) when both centers are projected vertically to the load waterline (LWL). This distance is known as "lead," and is usually expressed as a percentage of the waterline length. (See figure 1.)

If the CE is too far aft in relation to the CLP, a heavy weather helm will result; the boat will try to round up into the wind and can only be kept on course with difficulty. If the CE is too far forward (too much lead) the boat will develop lee helm; tacking will be difficult and she may jibe accidentally with serious and dangerous results.

At first thought, it might appear that a boat will balance best if her CE and CLP are vertically in line (no lead). However, calculations for CE and CLP are based on their geometric centers of area and it is obvious that these are not the true centers of pressure of the boat when it is heeled and moving.

Consider that, as the boat heels and the sheets are eased, even the geometric center of the sails moves forward and to leeward while the true aerodynamic CE is well forward of the geometric center due to the aerofoil shape of the sail. It will even vary with the amount of camber in an individual sail. The true hydrodynamic center of lateral pressure of the hull is also going to be well forward of the geometric CLP when the boat is close hauled, and will move aft as she bears away.

It is impossible to obtain the hydrodynamic CLP without costly tank testing and it is very difficult to obtain even an approximation of the true CE. For this reason, geometric centers are used in the design, and the architect compensates for any

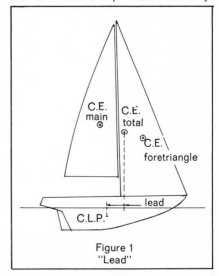

Figure 1
"Lead"

inaccuracies by giving the CE a certain amount of lead forward of the CLP.

Even tank testing does not always ensure perfect balance, for there are still many unknown factors. The most highly tested boats in the world are the America's Cup challengers and contenders. But even these boats have had their masts shifted, some often a considerable distance, after their trials in order to improve the balance.

The proper amount of lead depends on many factors and can range between 5 and 20% of the waterline length. The factors that affect the amount of lead, and their effect, are as follows:

Factors Shortening Lead

Short keel
Deep draft
Narrow beam
Stable hull
Fine forward waterlines
Low aspect ratio rig
Two masted rigs

Factors Lengthening Lead

Long keel
Shoal draft
Wide beam
Tender hull
Full forward waterlines
High aspect ratio rig
Single masted rigs

I do not have any absolute formula for the correct amount of lead. However, the suggested figures given in most books on the subject are too small in my opinion and they would tend to develop strong weather helm.

For example, one noted author gives a lead figure of 7-10% for a beamy ocean going cruiser with a long underwater profile. But I have seen a beamy, short keel yawl with 13% lead develop the most ghastly weather helm imaginable!

On the other hand, our 56′ Mystic (a beamy ocean going cruiser with long underwater profile) balances beautifully with 15% lead.

Another author recommends 5-7% lead for ketches and schooners, another thinks 3-4% is better. Ingenue, a 33′ schooner of our design, with a lead of 11.5%, developed enough weather helm so that the foretriangle area was enlarged 10% in order to correct it.

Bill Luders feels modern boats are rarely bothered by lee helm and can be given a long lead without problem. I am in complete agreement with him. While a modern beamy hull may stand quite a long lead, a too short lead is guaranteed to produce a ferocious weather helm.

As a guide to my students in the Yacht Design Institute, I suggest the following — start with about 12% to 14% lead and subtract 1% for every characteristic listed above under Factors Shortening Lead, and add 1% for every one listed under Factors Lengthening Lead.

Admittedly this is not a very scientific rule to go by, but the whole story of proper lead and balance boils down to intelligent guessing based on previous experience. There seems to be no way to pin it down any closer than that.

Based on the foregoing guide, a beamy (+1%), short keel (−1%), deep draft (−1%), heavily ballasted (−1%) sloop (+1%) with fine forward waterlines (−1% and a high aspect ratio rig (+1%) would wind up with about an 11% lead.

Similarly, a beamy (+1%), long keel (+1%), shoal draft (+1%), lightly ballasted (+1%) ketch (−1%) with full forward waterlines (+1%) and a low aspect ratio rig (−1%) would be given about 15% lead.

In actuality, even those results may be too small and our tendency when designing a sailplan would be to accept a slightly longer lead than is derived from the above, but never a shorter one.

A sailor who wishes to check the lead of his own vessel can do it quite simply.

The fastest and most accurate

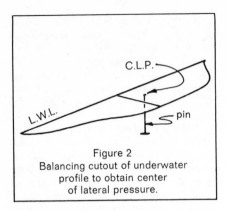

Figure 2
Balancing cutout of underwater
profile to obtain center
of lateral pressure.

method is to make a scale drawing of the underwater profile up to the LWL. Cut it out and balance it on a pin or divider point. The point where it balances is the CLP (See figure 2.)

When drawing the lateral plane, it is common practice to use only the forward half of the rudder area although some designers use all of it. A few, however, eliminate it completely. I use the half rudder, so bear in mind that these lead suggestions are based on this practice.

Calculating Center of Effort

To locate the CE of a triangular mainsail draw a line on the sailplan from mid-length on the foot to the head, then from the mid-length of the luff to the clew. (See figure 3.) Where the lines intersect is the CE. (The area of the roach is usually ignored for purposes of calculation.)

Use the same system to find the CE of the foretriangle. Make a line from the forward end of the foretriangle on deck to a point half way up the foretriangle hoist. Then make another line from the top of the foretriangle to a point half way between the mast and the forward end. Again the point of intersection is the CE.

Having found the mainsail CE (CE_m) and foretriangle CE, and knowing the areas of each, the location of the total CE (CE_T) can be found by drawing a line from the main CE to the foretriangle CE and

measuring its length (L). Then Distance CE_T from CE_m =

$$\frac{\text{Foretriangle area} \times \text{L}}{\text{Total area main and foretriangle}}$$

The CE and area of the foretriangle is used if genoa jibs are to be set. But if only a working jib is carried, its CE and area may be used instead of that of the foretriangle used in the above calculations. If two or more headsails are carried, as on a Friendship sloop, it becomes a matter of choice whether to use the foretriangle area and CE, or to figure the area and CE of each headsail and work out a common center for them using the method described above.

In any case, the areas of such light weather sails as mizzen staysails, fisherman staysail, jib or main topsails, etc., are usually ignored in working out a sailplan's overall area and CE.

When a designer has calculated the lead based on a trial sailplan, he can alter it if it is incorrect by shifting masts, sails, lengthening or shortening bowsprits, booms, etc., or whatever.

Changes to the lateral plane are made only rarely, for the lines may be completed by the time the final sailplan is worked out.

The owner with an actual balance problem is not so lucky, for a change is going to require more than just an eraser or a fresh sheet of tracing paper. If you feel your boat has a balance problem, first compute the lead as I have outlined, or have an architect do it if you are not confident in your own ability.

Then compare the percent of lead with the descriptive information given earlier in the article. Also look at similar designs published in SAIL and other sailing periodicals to establish that you in fact do have a lead problem. I mention this for I have seen a bad helm caused by warped rudders, centerboards, skegs and other factors that won't be af-

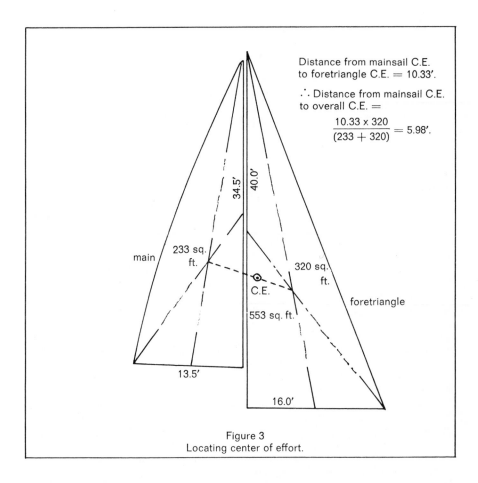

Distance from mainsail C.E. to foretriangle C.E. = 10.33'.

∴ Distance from mainsail C.E. to overall C.E. =

$$\frac{10.33 \times 320}{(233 + 320)} = 5.98'.$$

34.5'

40.0'

main

233 sq. ft.

320 sq. ft.

C.E.

foretriangle

553 sq. ft.

13.5'

16.0'

Figure 3
Locating center of effort.

fected by altering the lead.

If you know what the trouble is with your lead you can, within reasonable limits, alter it as follows:

To shorten lead (move CE aft, decrease lee helm)
-increase mast rake
-shorten bowsprit
-move mast(s) aft
-move centerboard forward

To lengthen lead (move CE forward, decrease weather helm)
-plumb up the mast(s); tilt them forward if necessary
-lengthen bowsprit or add a short sprit
-move mast(s) forward
-recut main and/or mizzen making it shorter on the foot
-move centerboard aft

Any problems that cannot be corrected by following these guidelines may involve a major rig change or an alteration to keel shape, rudder, centerboard shape or location. In most cases an architect's advice should be sought.

The end result of your changes and experimenting should produce a weather helm of 2-4°. If you can achieve this, you may find your boat taking on new life with regard to performance and ease of handling. It is well worth the little effort it takes and you should get plenty of thanks from your helmsmen; particularly ones who have been used to fighting a runaway weather helm!

Power Plants
and Auxiliary Sailboats

The usual U.S. auxiliary is horribly over-engined by European standards and it is interesting to note that this trend is now being reversed by the growing availability of light, low powered diesel engines suitable for installation in all but the smallest of craft.

A boat that might have had a 30 hp gasoline engine is now being fitted with a 12-15 hp diesel. Of course, the reason for this is not that owners have suddenly realized their boats cannot use 30 hp; rather it is because they want diesel power and the only engine that will fit into the hull is one of the small horsepower models. Still it is a healthy reversal of past practice.

Auxiliaries have always posed a problem in powering as the hull form required of a displacement sailboat is not one that lends itself to high speeds under power. The practical maximum speed of any displacement hull lies at a speed/length ratio of 1.34 (1.34 times the square root of the waterline length), and for economical powering of the average sailing hull, a speed/length ratio of 1.0 to 1.1 is to be preferred.

Both designers and owners add to the problem though by wanting the minimum of drag under sail, and the aperture and propeller are made as small as possible in order to reduce turbulence. The small propeller is further fitted with narrow blades to cut drag even more. And the end result is that the blade area is simply not enough to efficiently transmit the power of the relatively large engine.

Where maximum performance under power is desired, the answer is to fit the largest diameter 3-blade propeller possible, and accept the penalty of drag under sail.

To turn this large propeller, the shaft speed must be slowed by reduction gears to the proper speed for the propeller size and of course the engine must be of adequate power for the size of the boat.

All this will result in the greatest possible efficiency under power. But it is not likely to be a setup favored by the average sailing man.

Strangely enough, the owner of an outboard powered auxiliary can obtain efficient use of power, for the popular British Seagull outboards are geared extremely low and can turn large diameter wheels with good blade area.

Their 6.5 hp model turns an 11" five-blade propeller and this is not far off the size of wheel fitted to the average 25-30 hp direct drive gas engine. Of course, drag under sail is not a problem for an outboard owner —he simply tilts up or removes the engine when it is not in use.

The owner of an inboard powered auxiliary can't shuck off his propeller drag so easily, however, and he must compromise between efficiency under power and efficiency under sail.

He can achieve both, but only if he is willing to accept a small horsepower engine and the lower speeds that go with it. If the shaft rpm is kept reasonable, such an engine will turn the usual auxiliary sized propeller with good efficiency.

This efficiency will translate into decreased fuel consumption and smaller tanks can then be carried. This means less weight in fuel and more in the ballast keel; another boost to performance under sail.

Let's take an average auxiliary and make some comparisons. Our mythical boat is 25. feet LWL and has a 5.5 ton (12,300 lbs.) displacement. We'll fit it with two different engines. The first produces 20 shaft hp @ 2500 rpm. In theory this will power us to a speed/length (S/L) ratio of 1.35, or 6.7 knots *if* it is fitted with a large, efficient propeller.

This requires at least a 2:1 reduction gear and a 19-20" wheel. If we estimate fuel consumption as one gallon per hour (GPH) per 10 shaft horsepower, we would use two GPH and achieve a gas mileage of 3.85 miles per gallon, or about 97 miles on a 25 gallon tank.

On the other hand, if we fit a 12 shaft hp engine, our theoretical speed only drops to 6 knots, our mileage per gallon increases to 5.75 and we need only 17 gallons of fuel for the same cruising range.

The fuel saving alone is 50 lbs. in weight, and when this is added to the lighter engine and smaller tank, will mean possibly another 150 lbs. of ballast that may be put down where it counts.

To top it off, our 12 hp engine gives us the lower resistance of a smaller propeller, still another advantage.

Of course, we could fit the big engine with direct drive so it might turn a smaller wheel. But then efficiency would fall off drastically; speed is reduced and so is our cruising range. We would have lost a lot and gained nothing.

Folding propellers are common on our modern crop of fin keel boats and they could be a boon to owners if the builders would fit a reduction gear. Then a prop of efficient size could be used and the performance potential of a larger engine realized.

Unfortunately, the rule still seems to be *large engine, direct drive, small prop and inefficiency.*

My own feeling is that auxiliaries should be powered for speed length ratios of .9 to 1.15, a spread that includes the lower end of the scale for racing yachts and the higher end for cruisers.

Long distance offshore cruisers that need their engine rarely but require the maximum fuel economy should also consider settling for the lower speed-length ratios.

The enclosed table gives approximate engine BHP requirements for displacement yachts of various sizes and speeds. The power figure allows for a 30% loss in the engine accessories and shafting, and is based on a propeller efficiency of .55.

I can see a rush of letters from irate owners who will say their boat has twice the power shown on the chart and will barely make the noted speed. The obvious answer is that the propeller is not up to the job for reasons of too high a shaft speed, too small a blade diameter or a combination of other factors influencing its efficiency.

Of course, no power calculations are infallible and the table can be no more than a rough guide. Even identical hulls with identical engine and power train setups may vary considerably in speed potential due to differences in bottom smoothness, load, engine tuning, trim, etc.

Any sailor considering repowering would do well to consult a Naval Architect instead of simply having a yard replace his present engine with Brand X.

If he considers first what he wants to achieve with the new engine (i.e., maximum speed under power, fuel economy, minimum drag under sail, etc.) and provides the architect with the data necessary for an intelligent appreciation of the problem he will be well on his way to an efficient installation.

(S/L RATIO IN BRACKETS)

LWL	TONS DISP.	5 (KTS)	6 (KTS)	7 (KTS)	8 (KTS)	9 (KTS)
20 feet	1.5	4.0 (BHP)	8.0 (BHP)			
	2	4.5	11.0			
	3	5.5	16.5			
	4	7.0	23			
		(1.12)	(1.34)			
25 feet	4	5.5	12			
	5	7.0	16.5			
	6	8.0	22			
	7	9.5	29.5			
		(1.0)	(1.2)			
30 feet	6	5.0	12	26		
	8	5.5	15.5	36		
	10	6.5	19	47		
	12	7.5	23	60		
		(.91)	(1.1)	(1.28)		
40 feet	12	6.5	15	29	55	
	14	7.0	16.5	33	63	
	16	7.5	18	37	70	
	18	8.0	19	41	81	
	20	8.5	20.5	45	90	
	25	9.5	22	50	102	
		(.80)	(.95)	(1.11)	(1.26)	
50 feet	20	8.5	16.5	34	56	96
	25	9.0	18	41	68	119
	30	9.5	19	46	78	144
	35	11	20.5	51	87	168
	40	13	24	59	100	194
		(71)	(.85)	(.99)	(1.13)	(1.27)

— Figures to nearest .5 BHP
— Propeller efficiency taken at .55
— Allowance made for 30% power loss
  in engine and shafting.

— Assumption is made that hull form is
  correct for the indicated speed.

34

Cruising Auxiliaries

20-Ft. Sloop PHIALLE

```
SPECIFICATIONS:
LOA.................20'-0"
LWL.................17'-3"
BEAM................6'-9"
DRAFT..(C/B dn 6-0)..2'-2"
DISPL............ 2100 LBS
BALLAST............600 LBS
SAIL AREA........198 SQ FT
POWER (outboard)...6-10 HP
FUEL..............4-6 GALS
WATER.............10 GALS
CONSTRUCTION....MARINE PLY
PRISMATIC COEFF...... .537
```

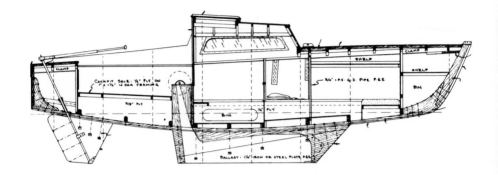

The *Phialle* class sloop (an ancient Greek word for a small drinking vessel) was designed as a small cruiser for the amateur builder, featuring a roomy cockpit for daysailing, with accommodations adequate for short cruises. There are three berths (for a real gain in comfort and elbow room, over four berths, in a boat this size), galley, ample stowage for sails and lines, and a watertight, self-bailing cockpit.

The framing consists of five marine plywood bulkheads reinforced with 1″ x 2-½″ oak. Keel and stem are oak. Planking and decks are ⅜″ marine plywood. Fastenings are glue and Anchorfast bronze nails. Ballast keel is two steel plates with space between for the steel centerboard—thus avoiding an expensive casting.

The rig consists of a hollow spruce box spar, stainless and dacron wire and rope. The modern ¾ rig insures performance and strength.

Bulkhead construction is strong, light, and watertight. She is simple to build and easy to maintain. No inboard engine was contemplated, but a small outboard can be fitted to the transom on a bracket, if desired.

Contact the designer for cost of study plans and construction blueprints.

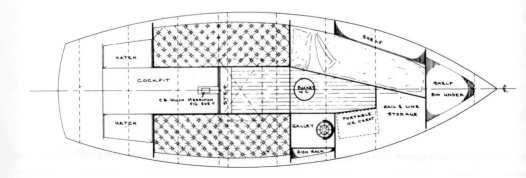

21⁻ Ft. Catboat CAPE COD

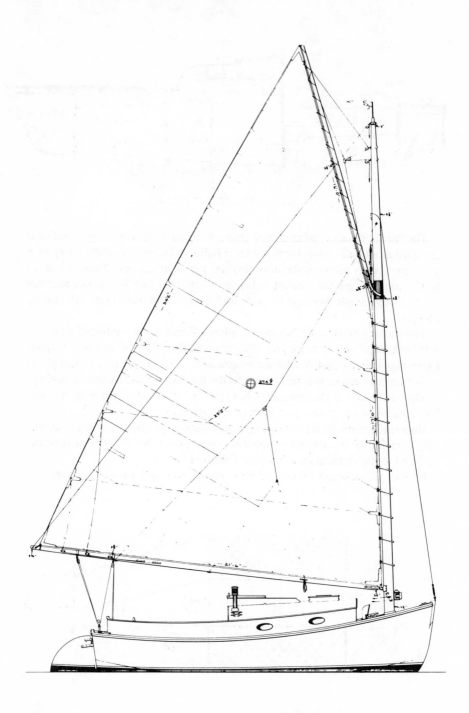

```
SPECIFICATIONS:
LOA................21'-7"
LWL................20'-0"
BEAM...............10'-0"
DRAFT..............2'-3"
DISPL............5850 LBS
BALLAST..........1600 LBS
SAIL AREA.......374 SQ FT
POWER (INBD)......5-10 HP
FUEL.............20 GALS
WATER............20 GALS
CONSTRUCTION...MARINE PLY
PRISMATIC COEFF.... .558
```

A chine version of the popular Cape Cod catboat, the design for *Cape Cod* was prepared as a simple-to-build modification of the famous type. She provides quite comfortable accommodations for her length. The spacious cockpit can easily accommodate two under a boom tent for family cruising, or seat a daysailing party of eight.

Construction is on the husky side, with commercial-size 2″ x 4″ frames, and heavy marine plywood planking for strength, durability, and simplicity of building. There is nothing in this design that cannot easily be handled by the competent amateur builder.

Power is supplied by a small, husky inboard with a 20-gallon fuel tank, sufficient for many hours of running under power. Any engine of 5-10 HP will be ample to drive her at good speed.

Tremendous stability is inherent in the beamy catboat hull, and she has ample sail area to move her along in any weather. All halyards lead to the cockpit to reduce the need for going forward to handle sail, and there are deep reefs to shorten sail in heavy going.

The cruising man who requires an able, comfortable, and simple-to-build cruising boat would do well to give a catboat serious consideration.

Here's a gratifying report from one owner: "I sailed out to the Dry Tortugas at the end of May. The round trip was approximately 500 miles. The boat sails fine and I am well satisfied. On the trip the seas ran about ten feet high, but the boat gave a feeling of security at all times. Thank you for the accommodating assistance you have offered, and for a fine boat." — *T. W. L.*, Clearwater, Florida.

Contact the designer for price of study plans or construction blueprints.

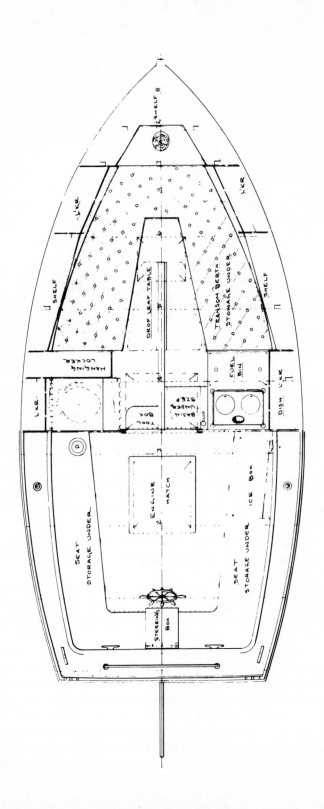

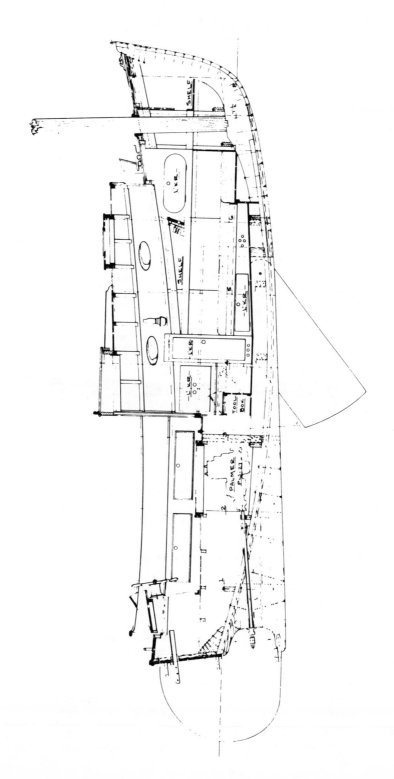

22-Ft. Ketch GRAND BANKS 22

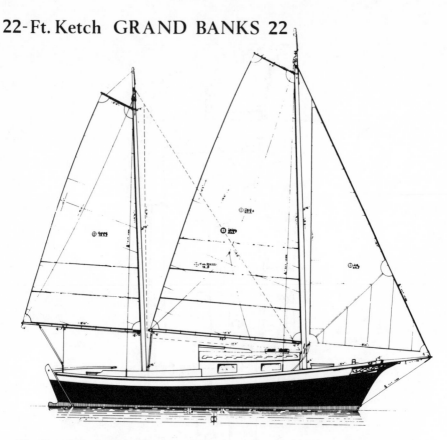

The *Grand Banks 22* is a husky small cruiser, designed for the owner desiring an attractive boat with good family accommodations, with an easily handled rig and a large cockpit for daysailing.

The dory is the simplest type of boat to build, yet it combines seaworthiness and sailing performance in a hull which avoids the boxy appearance of many plywood craft. Construction is of marine plywood or seam-batten carvel planking, glued and nail-fastened to bulkhead framing. This is very strong, light, and durable and, because of its simplicity, an ideal method for the amateur builder.

Seaworthiness and stability are assured by the well-flared topsides, self-bailing cockpit, and heavy outside ballast keel. The boat is instantly self-righting if laid over by a sudden squall, and the ketch rig can be reefed to handle any combination of wind and sea.

Auxiliary power is provided by a 3-5 outboard motor fitted in an enclosed well just abaft the cockpit, thus eliminating the need for an unsightly motor bracket or "kicker pit."

The rig is strong and easily handled, spreading ample sail area for light weather. Spars are spruce, and rigging is stainless steel wire and dacron rope.

The layout below provides three full-sized berths, galley, W. C., and ample stowage space for vacation cruises.

Contact the designer for cost of study plans and construction blueprints.

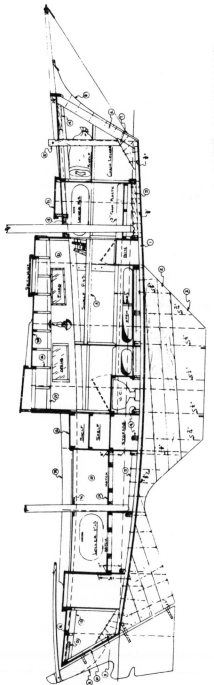

SPECIFICATIONS:
```
LOA.....................22'-0"
LWL.....................19'-2"
BEAM.....................7'-3"
DRAFT....................3'-0"
DISPL................2950 LBS
BALLAST...............875 LBS
SAIL AREA..........263 SQ FT
POWER (O/B)............5-9 HP
FUEL.................4-6 GALS
WATER................10 GALS
CONSTRUCTION...PLYWOOD OR WOOD
```

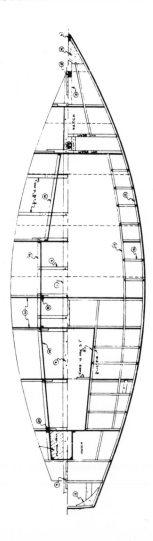

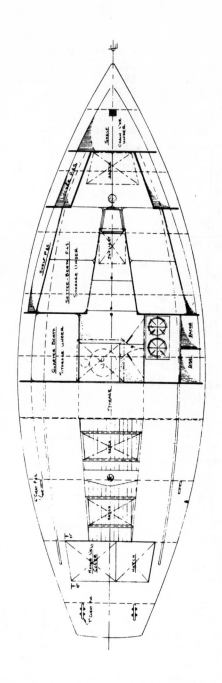

25-Ft. Catboat CHAPPAQUIDDICK

```
SPECIFICATIONS:
LOA...............25'-3"
LWL...............24'-0"
BEAM..............12'-0"
DRAFT.............3'-0"
DISPL.........10,100 LBS
BALLAST (INSIDE).2000 LBS
SAIL AREA......522 SQ FT
POWER (INBOARD)...8-30 HP
FUEL.............25 GALS
WATER............25 GALS
CONSTRUCTION........WOOD
PRISMATIC COEFF...  .529
(Vee bottom plywood ver-
 sion also available)
```

The catboat *Chappaquiddick* was designed for conventional construction; that is, carvel planking on steam-bent white oak frames with a husky white oak backbone. She is a heavy and solidly built vessel offering tremendous stability.

The accommodations offer two upper berths, two extension settee berths, a coal stove and a complete galley—with generous stowage space. The forepeak contains two hanging lockers and space for other gear.

The rig is traditional with solid spruce or pine spars and contains ample sail area for light weather conditions.

Auxiliary power is provided by a gas or diesel engine. There is space to fit most of the popular 8-30 HP models. Fuel and water tanks holds 25 gallons each.

This is one of the largest stock catboat plans available and the connoisseur of the type will appreciate the amount of thought that has gone into its design.

Contact the designer for cost of study plans or construction blueprints.

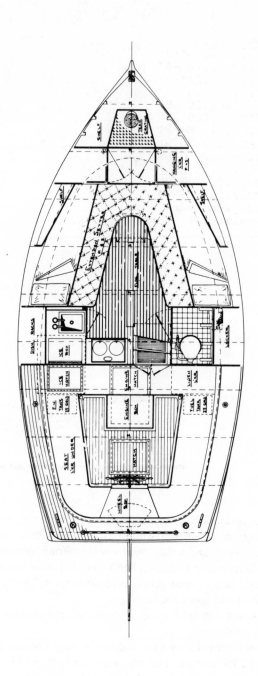

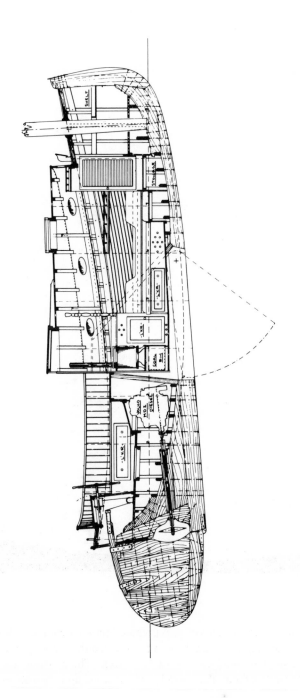

47

26-Ft. Eastport Pinky ALBERT HALLET

   This design, *Albert Hallet,* was prepared for the Penobscot Boat Works, which has been building a similar 32-ft. vessel called the Quoddy Pilot, and wanted to offer a a smaller, semi-custom yacht as well. The construction is similar to the methods used on their other model, and has stood up very well under years of hard sailing.

   The 26-ft. Lubec boat is designed primarily as a daysailer, with comfortable

```
SPECIFICATIONS:
LOA................25'-9"
LWL................22'-6"
BEAM................8'-9"
DRAFT...............4'-0"
DISPL..........11,500 LBS
BALLAST......... 4600 LBS
SAIL AREA.......460 SQ FT
POWER (DIESEL)...10-20 HP
FUEL.............20 GALS
WATER............40 GALS
CONSTRUCTION..GLASS/STRIP
```

cruising accommodations for one couple. She is based on the inshore sardine fishing boats of Maine, craft noted for good speed, great carrying capacity, and seaworthiness. Her heavy displacement assures an easy motion in a seaway, and the owner of the modern light-displacement fiberglass cruiser would find her as steady as a church in comparison.

The sail area is large for a 26-footer, but not out of keeping considering the displacement. However, the center of effort is low and the self-tending rig is simple to handle. Of course, many modern sailors might have to add some new skills to their repertoire to handle her since roller-reefing, turnbuckles, winches and other newfangled ideas have been eliminated for the sake of authenticity (and cost).

Plans are available for amateur builders, and the strip-planked construction should pose no special problems. Those desiring less daysailing space and more cruising room could shorten the cockpit and add the gained space to the interior. This could also be done on one of the professionally built craft from Penobscot Boat Works, as their vessels are built to order and can be modified to suit individual requirements.

The Lubec boat is an unusual vessel by modern standards, but will certainly win her share of praise wherever she sails. Incidentally, *Albert Hallet,* the name on her stern, was a well-known builder of the original working pinky sloops.

For further information, contact the designer, or Penobscot Boat Works, Rockport, Maine 04856.

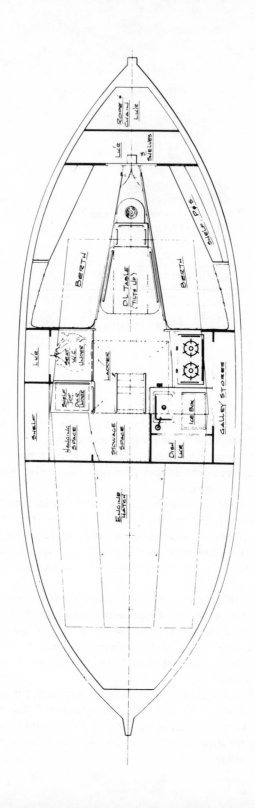

50

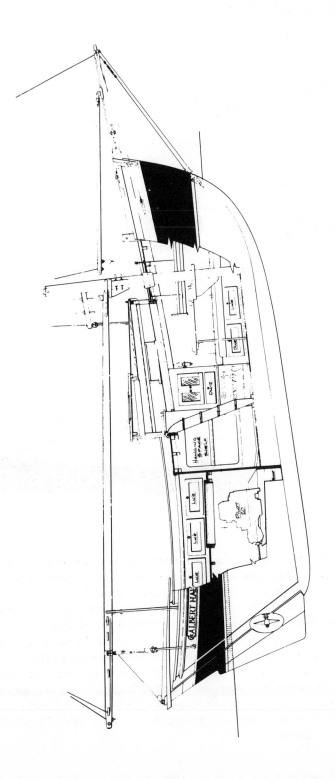

28-Ft. Sloop ALOHA

```
SPECIFICATIONS:
LOA...................27'-9"
LWL...................24'-6"
BEAM..................9'-5"
DRAFT.................4'-4"
DISPL...............6750 LBS
BALLAST.............2750 LBS
SAIL AREA...........374 SQ FT
POWER (GAS/DIESEL)...15-30 HP
FUEL.................18 GALS
WATER................35 GALS
CONSTRUCTION............FRP
PRISMATIC COEFF........ .49
```

The *Aloha 28* was designed as a fast cruiser, and with her long waterline, favorable sail and displacement ratios, and good stability, she performs very well. No attempt was made to fit her into any particular rating rule.

The layout was arranged to sleep four persons in comfort, and to provide the amenities required for pleasant cruising. Although a masthead sloop rig is standard, we provided an alternate cutter rig with boomed staysail for the cruising man who prefers to sail without the work involved in handling large genoas.

We selected an outboard rudder for several reasons: it is easy to inspect, simple to repair, and allows the longest possible waterline length. A skeg increases the rudder's efficiency, and assists in providing good tracking characteristics.

For further information, contact: Ouyang Boat Works, 1636 Charles St., Whitby, Ontario, Canada.

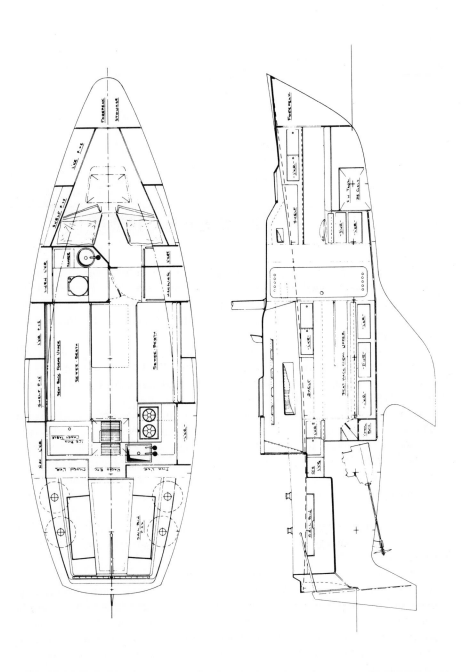

53

28-Ft. Ketch GRAND BANKS

The *Grand Banks 28,* like her smaller sister, is a salty little hooker, designed for the amateur builder, and has been well received, with several boats now building. She is available as a gaff sloop, ketch or schooner, or Bermuda ketch, to suit a variety of tastes. All rigs are designed to have the same Center of Effort so as to balance well.

Construction is simple but sturdy — ¾" marine plywood bottom planking, and ¾" carvel cedar topsides on sawn white oak frames. Decks are marine plywood or white pine. The cabin trunk is white pine with mahogany trim. Ballast casting is iron of 1750 lbs. Headroom is 5'-6".

Cruising accommodations are provided for four persons in two separate cabins with enclosed toilet and galley facilities, and ample stowage space. The self-bailing cockpit makes for comfortable daysailing.

The modified dory hull assures seaworthiness and an ability to take all kinds of weather. All in all, she is a boat that would appeal to the cruising man who is looking for a safe, economical and sensible auxiliary that will catch the eye in any harbor.

Power is provided by a Universal Atomic Four of 30 HP, or other engine of 10 HP and up to provide good cruising speeds, along with sufficient push to buck the heaviest seas.

Spars are solid spruce or pine, and the rigging is of galvanized wire and dacron rope — or manila for economy. Sail area is generous and eliminates the need for expensive genoa jibs in light weather. The working rig, without jib or topsail, provides ample canvas for normal winds, and deep reefs are shown for heavy weather conditions. Both ketch and schooner will handle well under a wide variety of reduced rigs, and are to be recommended where extensive coastal cruising is contemplated.

With her clipper bow, she is the kind of boat that looks salty and turns heads as she enters new ports.

For cost of study plans or construction blueprints, consult the designer.

SPECIFICATIONS:
```
LOA...............28'-7"
LWL...............24'-0"
BEAM..............8'-6"
DRAFT.............4'-6"
DISPLACEMENT......6000 LBS
BALLAST (KEEL)....1700 LBS
BALLAST (INSIDE)...400 LBS
SAIL AREA........440 SQ FT
POWER (GAS)........8-25 HP
FUEL............15-20 GALS
WATER...........15-20 GALS
CONSTRUCTION.......PLYWOOD
```

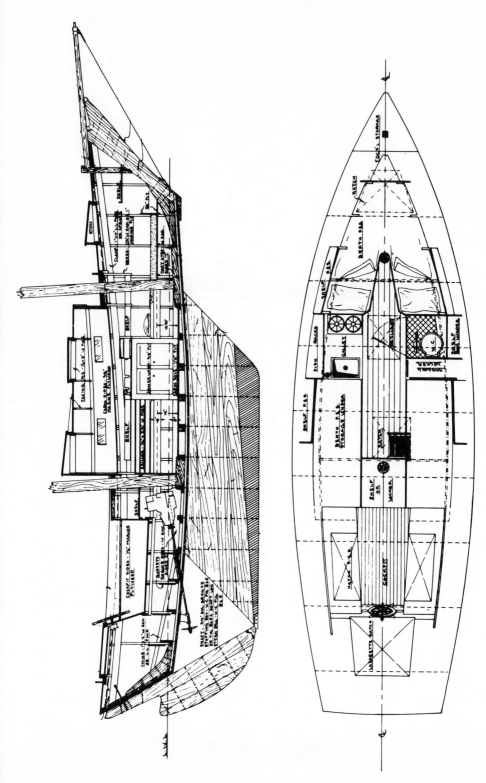

30-Ft. Ketch CARIB

Carib was designed for an owner who wanted a fast and comfortable ketch with accommodations for 5-6 persons. As the first boat was owner-built, the construction was developed with the amateur builder in mind, and consists of edge-nailed, glued-strip planking on bulkhead framing, fiberglass covered if desired. Decks and joinerwork are of marine plywood, fiberglass covered.

The double-headsail rig ketch is easy to handle, yet can spread over 600 sq. ft. of sail in light weather. Spars are aluminum. The sunken foredeck gives good security when handling headsails or ground tackle.

Accommodation include three permanent berths, plus two settee berths. An upper can be fitted to starboard if a six berths are required.

A variety of gas or diesel engines can be installed with 24-gallon fuel tanks, for a good cruising range. Steering is by wheel, although a tiller could be fitted if desired.

For anyone whose requirements call for a compact cruising auxiliary with excellent performance under sail, Carib is worthy of serious consideration. The clipper bow makes her attractive, a displacement of 10,000 lbs. insures easy handling, ground tackle will not be that hefty to handle and, with a modified layout below, she could as well serve as a moderate displacement, full-time live-aboard home for a man-and-wife crew.

Contact the designer for cost of study plans and construction blueprints. The Carib is also available in fibreglass from Cape Yachts Ltd., P.O. Box 6, Peng Chau, N.T., Hong Kong.

SPECIFICATIONS:
LOA................32'-4"
LOD................30'-4"
LWL................23'-3"
BEAM................9'-3"
DRAFT..............4'-8"
DISPLACEMENT......9800 LBS
BALLAST (KEEL)....3150 LBS
BALLAST (INSIDE)...350 LBS
SAIL AREA (KETCH)511 SQ FT
SAIL AREA (CUT.).465 SQ FT
POWER.............10-30 HP
FUEL..............24 GALS
WATER.............22 GALS
CONST.....GLASS OVER STRIP
PRISMATIC COEFF.... .549
(Available as production
 FRP boat from Hong Kong)

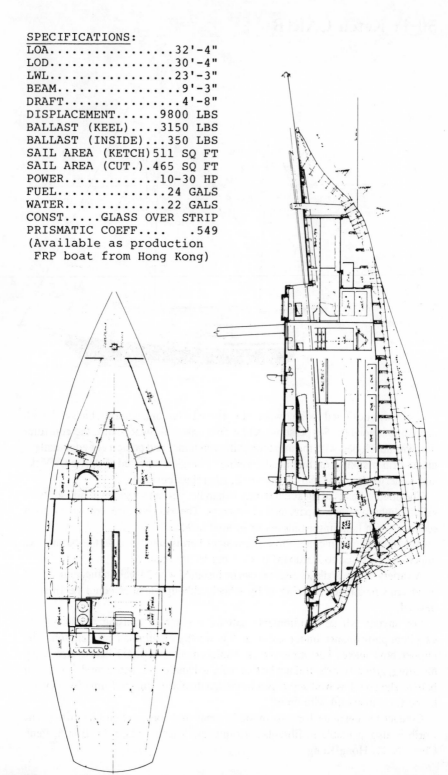

32-Ft. Schooner LAZYJACK

SPECIFICATIONS:
```
LOA...................31'-7"
LWL...................23'-9"
BEAM..................10'-8"
DRAFT (BD DN 6-6)......2'-10"
DISPLACEMENT.......12,500 LBS
BALLAST.............4000 LBS
SAIL AREA..........544 SQ FT
POWER (DIESEL).......20-40 HP
FUEL.................22 GALS
WATER................22 GALS
CONSTRUCTION.......FIBERGLASS
PRISMATIC COEFFICIENT.. .544
```

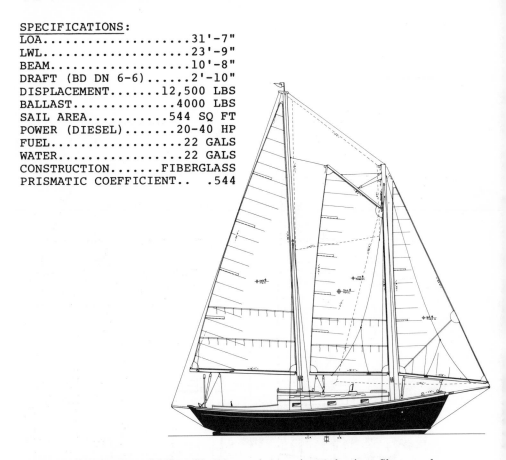

Lazyjack is perhaps the first fiberglass schooner in production. She was designed for her builder, who requested a husky, shoal-draft schooner for the man who wants a comfortable cruiser with no pretensions of beating a handicap rule. The vessel has ample sail area and should prove fast, and yet be easily handled. With the club jib set, no sheets need be tended, and the open layout below can sleep 4-5 persons for extended cruises. There is generous stowage space throughout, as befits a cruising boat. The shoal draft will let her slip into many thin anchorages.

Construction is of fiberglass with balsa-cored decks and trunk roof. Spars are aluminum, with standing and running rigging of stainless steel wire and dacron rope.

The galley, as shown, has a two-burner stove, sink, and 10 cu. ft. icebox, in a midship location favored by many.

The large cockpit is ideal for daysailing parties, and diesel power will insure that she will reach her owner's intended port regardless of light winds on those flukey summer days found in so many areas on the East Coast.

For further information on this design, contact the builder: Ted Herman, 3631 Ocean Avenue, Seaford Harbor, NY 11783.

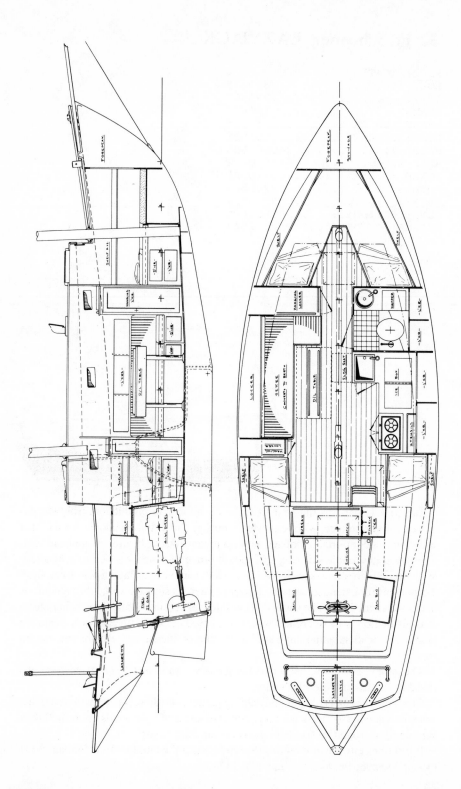

32-Ft. Sloop DOUGLAS

The *Douglas 32* was one of our first production designs and is still in production. She has proven to be a good all-around performer, and is exceptionally fast in light weather.

The arrangement plan shows accommodations for 4-5 persons who will be berthed in comfort, and still provide plenty of the kind of stowage space needed on long cruises. One of these boats has completed two Atlantic crossings, and has established a reputation for seaworthiness and easy motion. Another boat proved her speed by winning a 150-mile long-distance race on the West Coast. However, she was not designed as a racing yacht, and her prime purpose is to serve as an able, fast, and easily handled family cruiser. As of this writing, over 50 of these boats have been built and, according to reports, are proving to be popular and successful with the families which own them — perhaps the best test there is of a design.

For more information, contact the designer, or the builder, Command Yachts (Int'l) Ltd., 875 Florence St., P.O. Box 2154, London, Ontario, Canada.

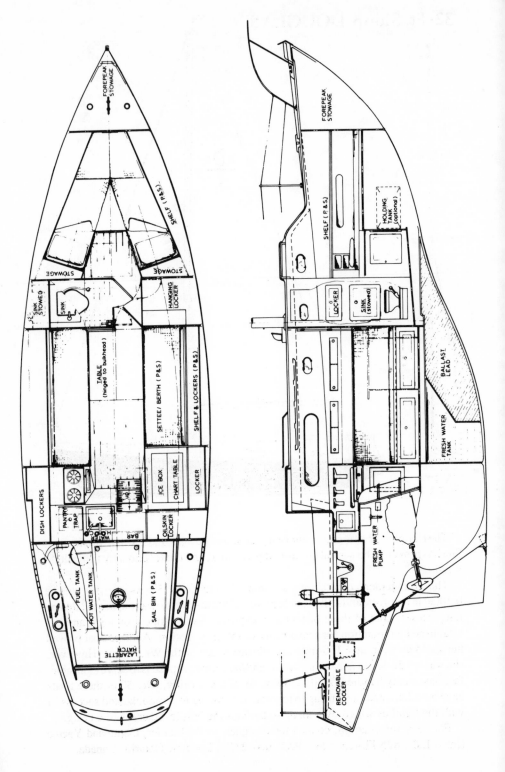

SPECIFICATIONS:
LOA.............31'-10"
LWL.............22'-9"
BEAM.............9'-3"
DRAFT.............4'-9"
DISPL........10,000 LBS
BALLAST (LEAD).4000 LBS
SAIL AREA.....460 SQ FT
POWER (DIESEL)....20 HP
FUEL............18 GALS
WATER...........40 GALS
CONSTRUCTION.FIBERGLASS
PRISMATIC COEFF.. .548

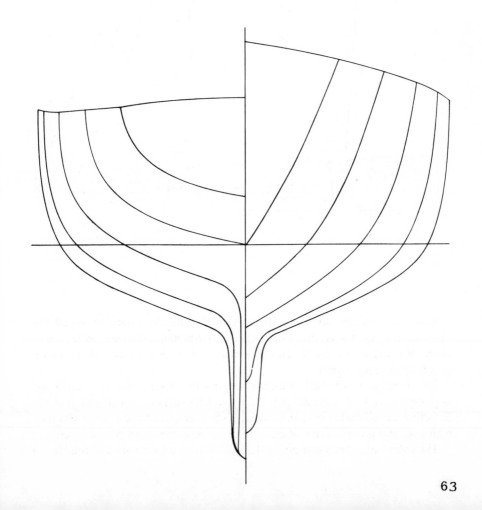

32-Ft. Ketch TERN

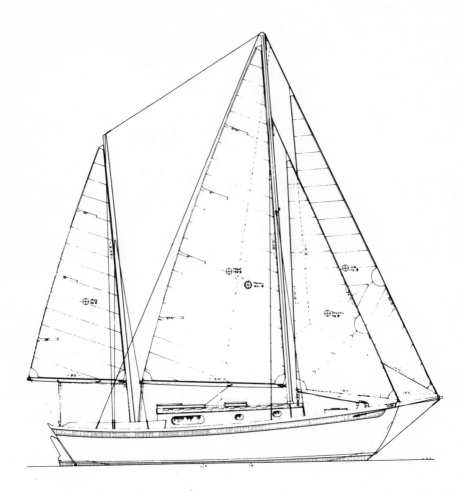

Tern is a seaworthy and comfortable ketch designed for extensive coastal and offshore cruising. The accommodations offer five berths, a complete galley, large chart table, and enclosed head. There is generous stowage space to suit her purpose as a long-distance cruiser.

The chine hull can be built of marine plywood or conventional carvel planking, as preferred, and the construction is ideally suited to the competent home builder. Scantlings are on the heavy side, producing a boat that will stand up to rough going with ease and provide years of cruising pleasure with normal maintenance.

The chine hull, generous beam and good ballast/displacement ratio combine to

```
SPECIFICATIONS:
LOA....................31'-10"
LWL....................26'-2"
BEAM...................10'-1"
DRAFT..................4'-7"
DISPL..............13,250 LBS
BALLAST (IRON).......4000 LBS
SAIL AREA...........501 SQ FT
POWER (GAS/DIESEL)...20-35 HP
FUEL..................40 GALS
WATER.................30 GALS
CONST (WOOD)....CARVEL OR PLY
PRISMATIC COEFF.......  .587
```

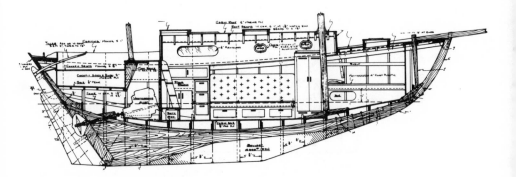

produce a stiff and weatherly boat. The versatile ketch rig enables her to reduce canvas in a blow and still retain a balanced helm. Spars are hollow spruce, and rigging is stainless steel wire and dacron rope.

Auxiliary power is provided by a husky gas or diesel engine of 20-35 HP, for cruising speeds of 6-6½ knots.

Tern is a vessel for the confirmed cruising man, a yacht that combines seaworthiness, sailing pleasure and cruising comfort in a rugged package.

The design fee, as with most other designs shown in this book, includes the right to build one boat, complete blueprints, extensive written specifications, plus any advice or special sketches or instructions required by the builder during construction. Contact the designer for cost of study plans or construction blueprints.

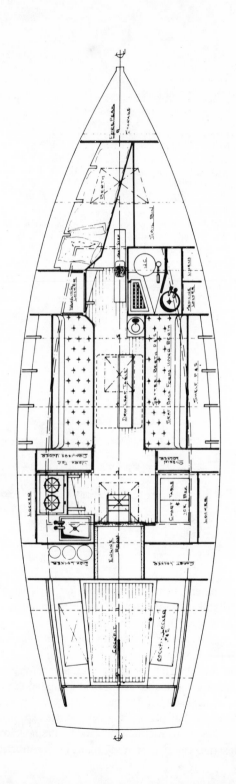

32-Ft. Sharpie Ketch MYSTIC

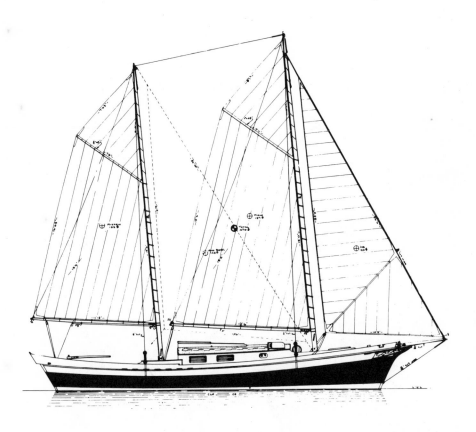

The sharpie ketch *Mystic* was drawn up to provide the amateur builder with a reasonably sized yacht of simple construction and low cost. She is built of marine plywood on white oak frames, glue- and nail-fastened for ease of construction, strength and watertightness.

She represents, we think, an improvement over the original working sharpies in that she has sufficient ballast to insure excellent stability, a self-bailing cockpit, and a double-ended hull with a high pinky stern — for safety in following seas.

The picturesque rig, resembling a gaff ketch with topsails set, was adapted from a Great Lakes working sharpie. It spreads ample sail area for light winds, yet has a low center of effort and the convenience of a single halyard for each sail.

The layout below provides four full-sized berths, generous stowage space, and complete facilities for extended cruising. For auxiliary power, an outboard of 7-12

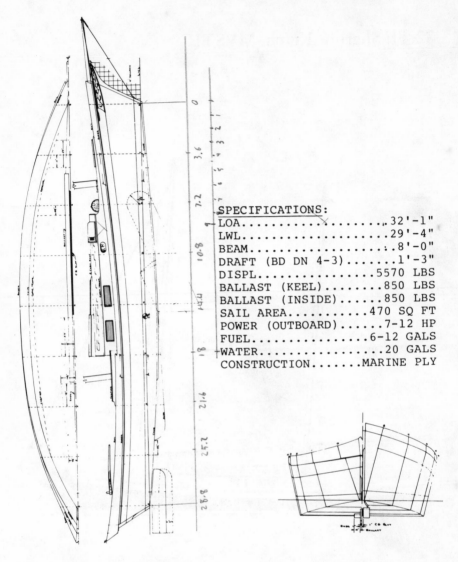

```
SPECIFICATIONS:
LOA..................32'-1"
LWL..................29'-4"
BEAM..................8'-0"
DRAFT (BD DN 4-3).......1'-3"
DISPL..............5570 LBS
BALLAST (KEEL)........850 LBS
BALLAST (INSIDE)......850 LBS
SAIL AREA...........470 SQ FT
POWER (OUTBOARD)......7-12 HP
FUEL................6-12 GALS
WATER................20 GALS
CONSTRUCTION.......MARINE PLY
```

HP, operating in a convenient centerline motor well, will serve well.

Mystic possesses all the advantages of the original sharpies; her shoal draft lets her slip into gunkholes and across sandbars forbidden to keel boats; she is easy to handle; she is inexpensive to build and maintain, yet seaworthy enough for coastwise cruising.

Dollar for dollar, she will repay her owner with more performance, comfort and cruising pleasure than any other type of sailboat he can build. In spite of all the fine writing done by Howard I. Chapelle on early American workboats adaptable to pleasure use, it seems a shame that more owners don't realize—before they build—that a boat like *Mystic* is just right for the kind of cruising they actually do, but instead build something else and then discover the truth about their cruising needs later.

For cost of study plans/construction blueprints, contact the designer.

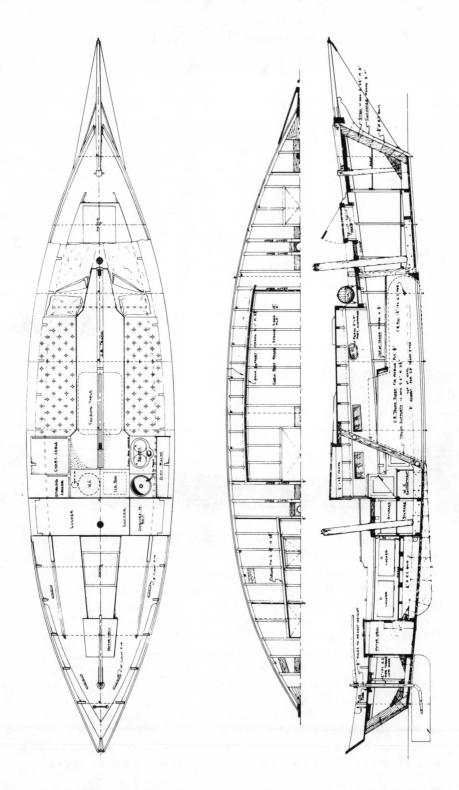

33-Ft. Staysail Schooner INGENUE

Ingenue is a fast, modern schooner designed for ocean racing and cruising. Accommodations provide six berths, separate chart table and berth for navigator, ample stowage space, enclosed toilet, compact galley and full headroom.

Construction has been kept simple for the backyard builder. Glued-strip planking eliminates the need for steam-bent frames, and makes for a strong, tight, one-piece hull. Plywood bulkheads are used for framing and arthwartship strength. Decks are ½-inch marine plywood, and cabinhouse and trim are mahogany. The keel and stem are of white oak, and fastenings are bronze.

The foresail schooner rig is easily handled for cruising, but spreads 900 sq. ft. of sail on a reach for racing. Spars are hollow Sitka spruce. The rigging is stainless steel wire and dacron rope.

The firm bilges, deep draft, and generous ballast assure a stiff and able boat that can keep going in heavy weather.

Auxiliary power is by a Universal Atomic Four of 30 HP, or equal, and will push the easily driven hull at a good clip, even against headwinds and in choppy seas.

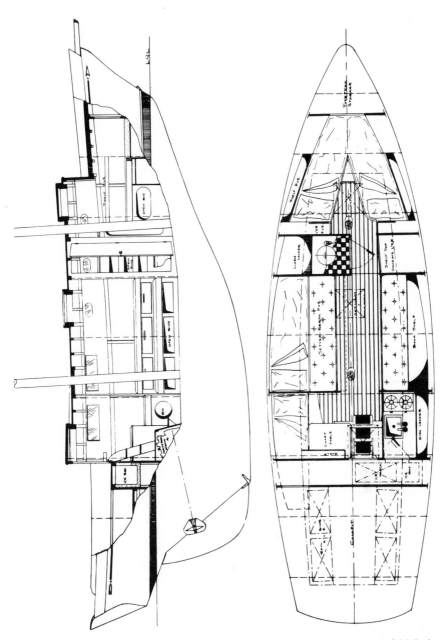

For a schooner, *Ingenue* has had an enviable racing record: 2nd (of 93 in her class) in 1966 Chicago-Mackinac; 1st to Finish & 1st Overall in 1966 Pensacola Race (300 mi.); 1st in Class D & 4th In Fleet (127 boats) in 1967 Tri-State; a First Overall, a Second-To-Finish, a Second-in-Class, and a Third-in-Class in the next two years in St. Pete-Naples, Tampa-Egmont Key, and St. Pete-Venice Races; First in Class B in 1969 St. Pete-Mexico (465 miles) as well as Second in Fleet; and First-in-Class in 1974 Mystic Schooner Race.

Contact the designer for cost of study plans and construction blueprints.

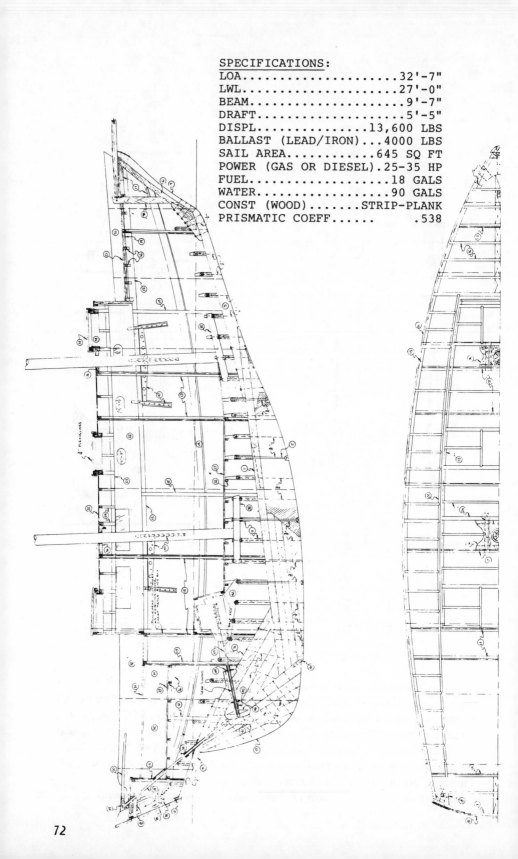

SPECIFICATIONS:
```
LOA.....................32'-7"
LWL.....................27'-0"
BEAM....................9'-7"
DRAFT...................5'-5"
DISPL..............13,600 LBS
BALLAST (LEAD/IRON)...4000 LBS
SAIL AREA...........645 SQ FT
POWER (GAS OR DIESEL).25-35 HP
FUEL...................18 GALS
WATER..................90 GALS
CONST (WOOD).......STRIP-PLANK
PRISMATIC COEFF......    .538
```

34-Ft. Sloop ALOHA

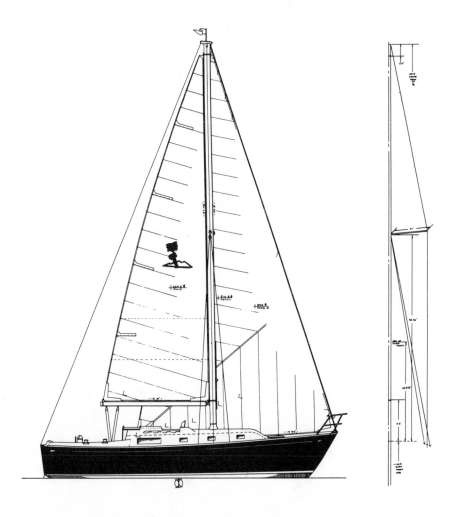

The *Aloha 34* is the second in a line of fast, fin-keel cruising yachts developed for Ouyang Boat Works, Ltd. With generous beam and a 40% ballast ratio she is fast and stable, while her deep draft assures good windward ability.

The accommodations are unusually good for a 34-footer, featuring a private entrance to the roomy head, four permanent berths, a very workable chart table area, spacious U-shaped galley, and a comfortable large cockpit. She can accommodate seven persons if required. This is a bit of a crowd for a 34-footer, although the racing owner may make use of all the berths sooner or later.

Although no particular attention was paid to the IOR rule when we designed her, we expect she will do well under an enthusiastic owner as she has many of the trademarks of the IOR boats.

For information contact OUYANG Boat Works, 1636 Charles St., Whitby, Ontario, Canada.

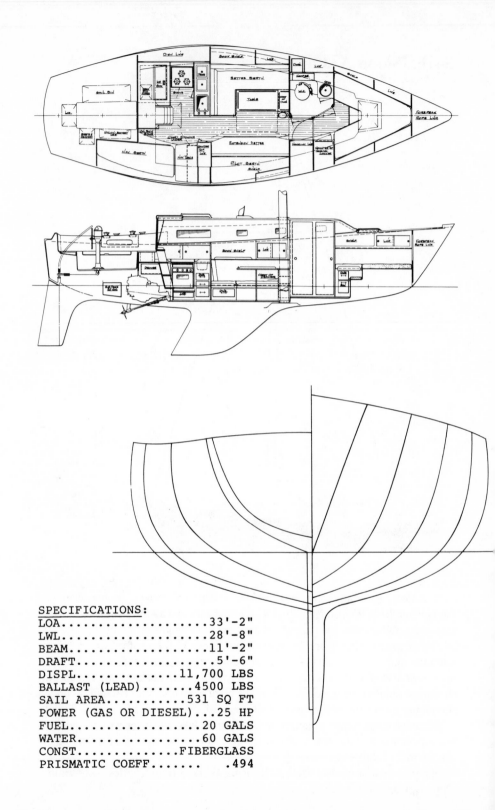

SPECIFICATIONS:

LOA....................33'-2"
LWL....................28'-8"
BEAM...................11'-2"
DRAFT...................5'-6"
DISPL.............11,700 LBS
BALLAST (LEAD).......4500 LBS
SAIL AREA..........531 SQ FT
POWER (GAS OR DIESEL)...25 HP
FUEL.................20 GALS
WATER................60 GALS
CONST.............FIBERGLASS
PRISMATIC COEFF....... .494

34-Ft. Pinky Sloop SUNSHINE

```
SPECIFICATIONS:
LOA..................34'-5"
LWL..................30'-4"
BEAM.................11'-4"
DRAFT................5'-0"
DISPL.............23,900 LBS
BALLAST (LEAD)......9000 LBS
SAIL AREA..........742 SQ FT
POWER (DIESEL).........40 HP
FUEL................100 GALS
WATER...............120 GALS
CONST.............FIBERGLASS
PRISMATIC COEFF......  .558
```

Mr. George Moffett commissioned the design of *Sunshine* out of an admiration for the Quoddy Pilot Boat built by the Penobscot Boat Works, but he required a larger boat and wanted her built of fiberglass. She is due to be launched in the summer of 1975.

The hull is of full-keel, heavy-displacement type, with a displacement/length ratio of 382. She promises to be quite comfortable and able in heavy going, and should have a steady helm and an easy motion. The Maine pinkies were noted for speed and seaworthiness, and this design should be no exception.

Her sail area/displacement ratio of 14.3 is a bit lower than we usually like to see, but is really determined by the maximum single sail that can be handled by a small crew, and we feel her 542 sq. ft. mainsail is the limit. However, the sail area/wetted surface ratio is still 2.0, so light weather performance will be quite acceptable, and in moderate to heavy breezes, she has the stability to carry full sail and really pick up her heels when other 35-footers are well reefed-down.

The hull was built using a one-off process in a "disposable" female mold developed by Dave Dana, and is unusually sweet and fair, with a minimum of fairing up required. The decks and trunk are built in one piece, using the same system, and have the non-skid molded in just as on a production yacht.

This design should provide a comfortable traditional cruising yacht that will turn heads in any port she enters. Plans are available for construction in any one-off-process—C-flex, Airex core, etc. Contact the designer for cost of study plans or construction blueprints, or contact the builder, Dave Dana, Box 161, Vineyard Haven, Mass. 02568, for data on bare hulls and deck castings.

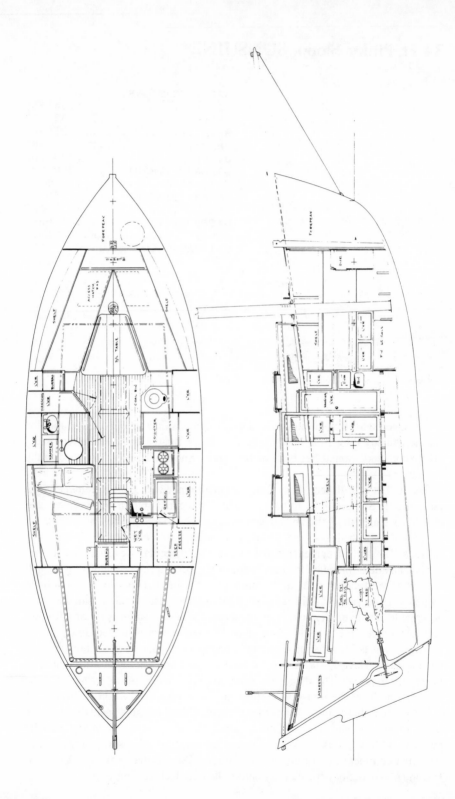

34-Ft. Cutter JASON

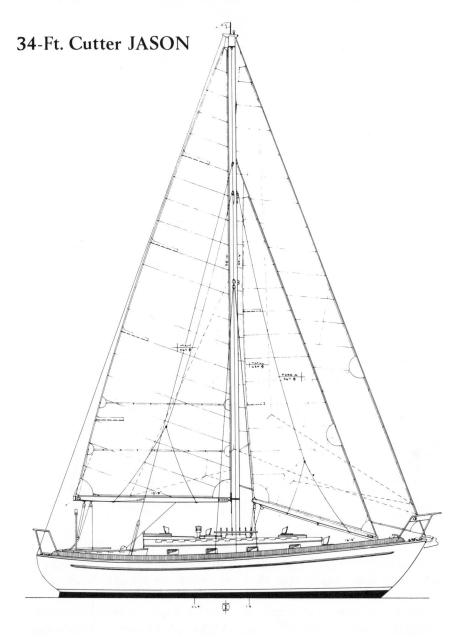

Jason was a custom design commission for a West Coast client who wanted a seaworthy long-distance cruiser, and knew, from experience, exactly what he needed in such a vessel. As a result, *Jason* has many features in her design that make her safer, easier to handle, and more comfortable — such as a small cockpit well, permanent boom gallows, running backstays, double head rig, exceptionally large saloon, and ample stowage space throughout.

Five dorade vents plus a skylight and eight opening ports will keep the interior livable even in the tropics, while there is a small cabin heater to remove the chill in colder climates.

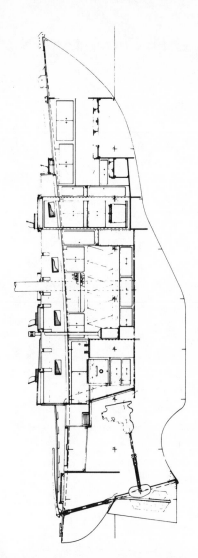

```
SPECIFICATIONS:
LOA...................34'-6"
LWL...................27'-4"
BEAM..................11'-2"
DRAFT..................5'-0"
DISPL..............16,800 LBS
BALLAST (LEAD).......6200 LBS
SAIL AREA...........634 SQ FT
POWER (DIESEL).......10-30 HP
FUEL.................27 GALS
WATER (3 TANKS).......95 GALS
CONST..............FIBERGLASS
PRISMATIC COEFF.......  .534
```

Auxiliary power is an economical 10 HP diesel with a 27-gal. fuel capacity, although a larger engine (and more fuel) would be possible. Water tankage amounts to 95 gallons in three tanks.

The layout shows four berths, plenty for long-distance cruising, but fitting uppers in the saloon would let her sleep six without major changes. There is ample beam to fit a pilot berth on the port side if desired.

Construction is of fiberglass, using Seeman C-Flex material as a basis. This is an ideal method for one-off construction, and is quite within the capability of a good amateur builder.

Anyone seeking a world cruiser, or simply a fast and seaworthy yacht for coastal cruising should find *Jason* a logical candidate. She is now in semi-production by Miller Marine Construction Co., Bainbridge, Washington 98110, and is being offered in several stages from bare hull to complete boat.

Contact the designer for cost of study plans or construction blueprints.

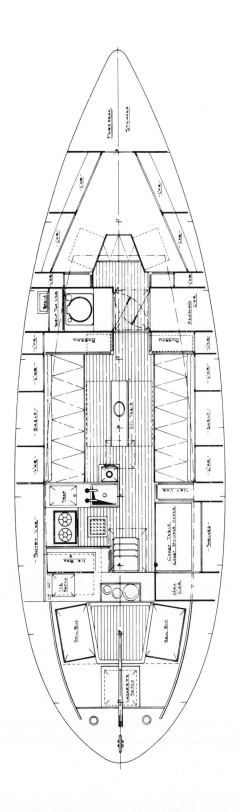

35-Ft. Cutter MB/S-35

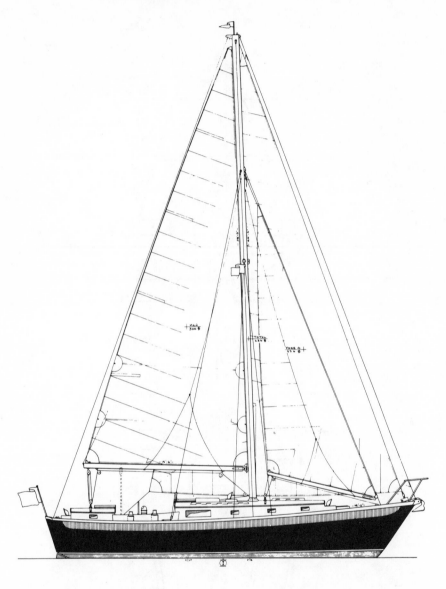

The *MB&S 35* was designed to provide the amateur builder with a modern, high performance and seaworthy cruiser that would be available as a stock plan. Construction is of glued-strip planking on bulkhead framing, and the hull is Vectra-sheathed to reduce maintenance. An alternate construction method calls for heavy laminations of fiberglass laid over a light wood skin. This method eliminates the need for the heavy keel timbers of the more traditional wood construction method, replacing it with a thick glass laminate. Decks in both construction methods are of fiberglass-covered marine plywood. She is available

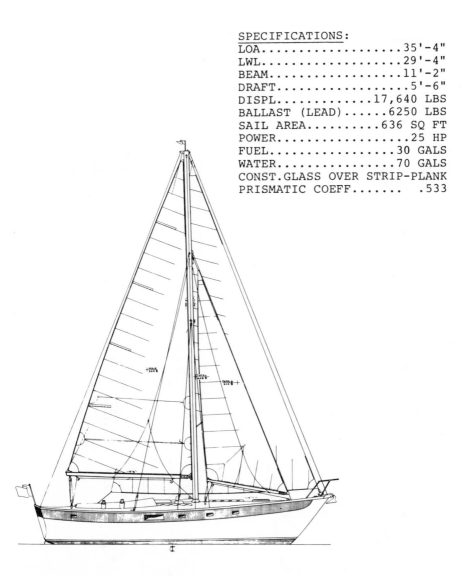

```
SPECIFICATIONS:
LOA..................35'-4"
LWL..................29'-4"
BEAM.................11'-2"
DRAFT.................5'-6"
DISPL............17,640 LBS
BALLAST (LEAD)......6250 LBS
SAIL AREA..........636 SQ FT
POWER................25 HP
FUEL................30 GALS
WATER...............70 GALS
CONST.GLASS OVER STRIP-PLANK
PRISMATIC COEFF.......  .533
```

with flush deck or trunk cabin.

The layout provides berths for 5-8 in three separate cabins but the boat is really intended as a live-aboard long distance cruiser for two persons, with occasional guests. The large galley, separate navigation area, general privacy and comfort are rarely found on yachts of this size and displacement. The cutter rig is fitted for its general handiness, and the mast is strongly stayed with running backstays and forestay, providing additional support.

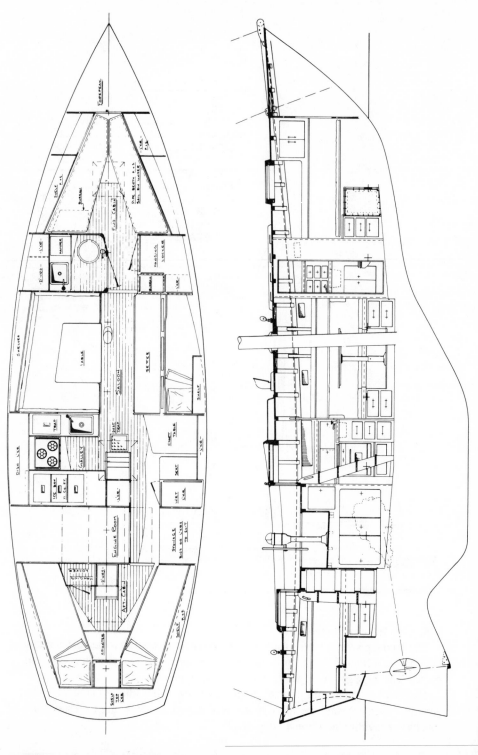

36-Ft. Sloop/Cutter CABOT

```
SPECIFICATIONS:
LOA.....................35'-7"
LWL.....................29'-8"
BEAM....................11'-8"
DRAFT...................4'-9"
DISPL...............15,000 LBS
BALLAST (LEAD)........5800 LBS
SAIL AREA............632 SQ FT
POWER (DIESEL)...........25 HP
FUEL..................30 GALS
WATER.................100 GALS
CONST......FIBERGLASS SANDWICH
PRISMATIC COEFF......    .553
```

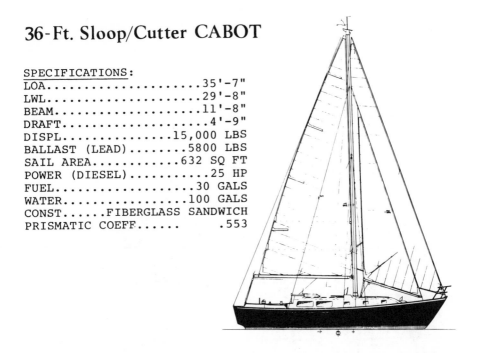

The *Cabot 36* was conceived as a long-distance cruiser. The hull incorporates a bustle for reduced resistance, and the rudder is mounted well aft to assure directional stability and a steady helm. The cutaway ahead of the rudder will, however, eliminate the hard-to-turn tendency often seen in long-keeled hulls. With a displacement-length ratio of 257 she should be easily driven, and a generous sail plan will insure good speeds even in light airs. In heavy going the wide beam and ample displacement-ballast ratio will provide good stability, making her dry on deck and comfortable. Sloop or cutter rig is available, many preferring the cutter with its self-tending staysails and the extra rig strength provided by the added forestay and runners.

The layout is fairly standard, but much thought has gone into making it workable and comfortable. There is generous stowage space and elbow room for extended cruising by two couples. Construction is of Airex foam and balsa-cored fiberglass, combining lightness and stiffness, good insulation, and durability.

The accommodation provides two berths, two bureaus, a hanging locker, and a private entrance to the head, up forward. The cockpit is T-shaped with sail bin, line lockers and lazarette. The galley-navigation area has a 3-burner stove, large icebox, oilskin space, chart table and navigator's berth. In the saloon the dinette is convertible to a double berth, plus extension settee, pilot berth, two hanging lockers and bureau.

The engine is a Volvo MD2B diesel of 25 HP, with fuel of 30 gallons and water of 100 gallons in two tanks. An Edson pedestal steerer is fitted; electrical system is 12 volt with 38 AH alternator on the engine. Spars are aluminum; winches are by Barlow.

Contact Cabotcraft Industries Ltd., P.O. Box 9000 Sydney, N.S., Canada, for further information.

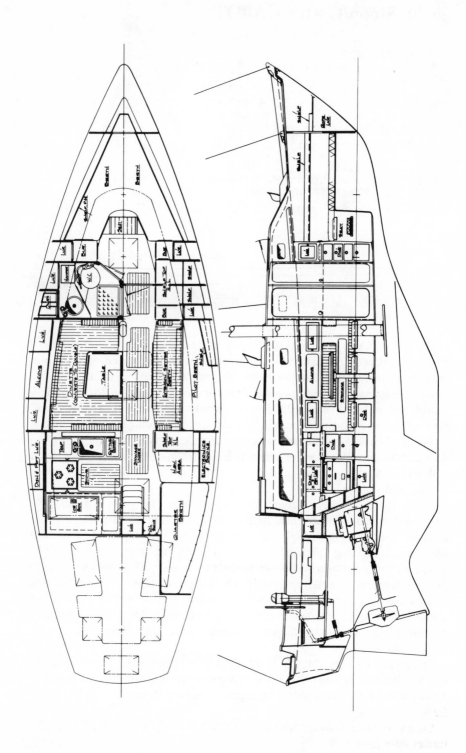

37- Ft. Ketch AMEE

SPECIFICATIONS:
```
LOA......................37'-5"
LWL......................31'-6"
BEAM.....................11'-4"
DRAFT (BD DN 8')..........4'-2"
DISPL................14,800 LBS
BALLAST (LEAD).........6000 LBS
SAIL AREA.............700 SQ FT
POWER (GAS OR DIESEL)...16-30 HP
FUEL....................40 GALS
WATER...................60 GALS
CONST.....GLASS OVER STRIP-PLANK
  (OR:  FIBERGLASS SANDWICH)
PRISMATIC COEFF........... .548
(Also available in a keel ver-
  sion with 6' draft fin, cutter
  rig, in foam-core FRP)
```

This design, the 37-foot Ketch *Amee,* was prepared for an owner who required a fast, shoal-draft yacht suitable for cruising and distance racing. The hull sections are very powerful, with hard bilges and widely flaring topsides, giving excellent sail-carrying power and reserve stability. The long waterline assures high average speeds and the ketch rig spreads ample sail area for all conditions.

Construction is of fiberglass-covered strip-planking, on bulkhead framing, with decks and cabin trunks of fiberglassed marine plywood — guaranteeing a strong, tight hull, with minimum maintenance. Spars are aluminum, with stainless steel and dacron rigging.

The accommodations are laid out to sleep seven in three separate cabins for privacy and comfort. The wide beam affords a feeling of spaciousness rarely achieved on a boat this size.

Auxiliary power is provided by a 16-30 HP gas or diesel engine, the original boat having a 2-cylinder Volvo diesel. Tankage is 40 gallons of fuel, and 60 gallons of water.

The yachtsman looking for a fast and comfortable cruiser might do well to give

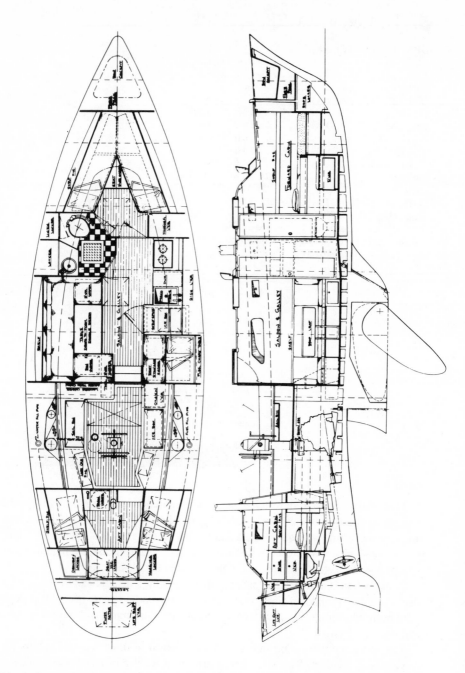

this design serious consideration. A new version now being designed for a West Coast owner will have a fin keel, 5'-7½" draft, cutter rig, and will be built of figerglass over Airex foam.

Contact the designer for cost of study plans and construction blueprints for either model described above.

FRIENDSHIP 38 Sloop

```
SPECIFICATIONS:
LOA.....................38'-8"
LWL.....................29'-6"
BEAM....................11'-10"
DRAFT...................5'-9"
DISPL...............19,850 LBS
BALLAST (LEAD)........6000 LBS
SAIL AREA.......939-1188 SQ FT
POWER (GAS OR DIESEL).25-36 HP
FUEL...................30 GALS
WATER..................40 GALS
CONST (WOOD).......STRIP-PLANK
```

The *Friendship 38* follows in the tradition of this much beloved native type, modified to improve performance without affecting her traditional appearance.

Changes include increased freeboard with outside ballast for added stability, a more efficient rudder shape, smoother fairing of the garboards, and a modification of the lateral plane shape for increased windward performance. The rig is tradi-

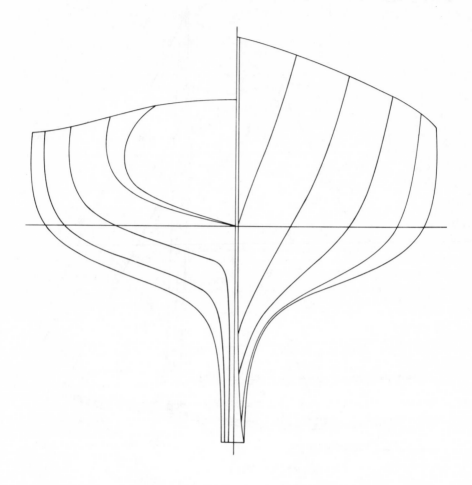

tional in appearance and arrangement.

Accommodations are simple, in keeping with her type, but there is generous stowage space and a couple could cruise for weeks in comfort. The roomy cockpit is ideal for daysailing.

Construction has been modernized slightly, and is of edge-glued strip-planking on steam-bent frames, bronze fastened. Decks and cabin trunk roof are of marine plywood.

The auxiliary specified is a 36 HP diesel, but a smaller model diesel or a gas engine in the 25-30 HP range could be substituted and would provide adequate power.

Those who love the Friendship sloop and want one that is large, fast, and solidly built, should find the *Friendship 38* of interest — a comfortable cruising auxiliary.

Contact the designer for cost of study plans or construction blueprints.

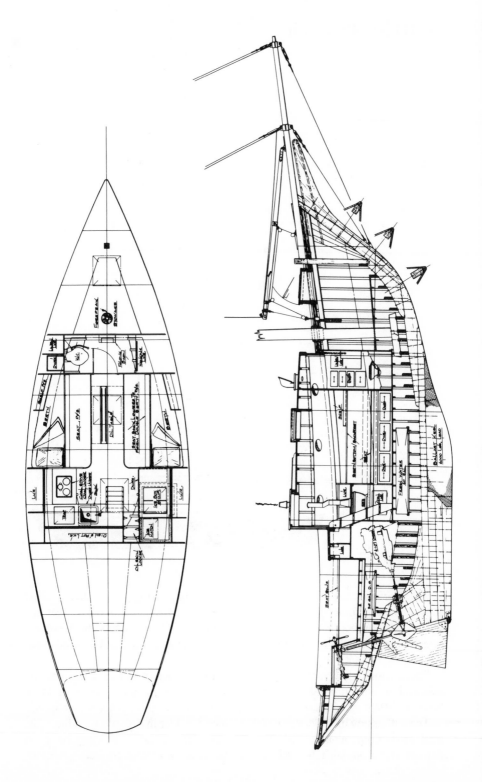

WHITBY 42 Ketch

```
SPECIFICATIONS:
LOA...................42'-0"
LWL...................32'-8"
BEAM..................13'-0"
DRAFT.................5'-0"
DISPL.............23,500 LBS
BALLAST............8500 LBS
SAIL AREA.........875 SQ FT
POWER (DIESEL)......40-80 HP
FUEL................300 GALS
WATER...............300 GALS
CONSTRUCTION.....FIBERGLASS
PRISMATIC COEFF......  .543
```

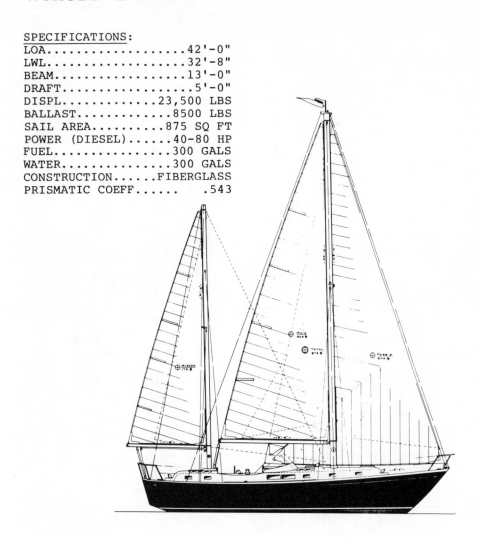

The *Whitby 42* was designed to provide a roomy cruising yacht with sufficient accommodation for living aboard on extended cruises. Shoal draft of five feet was selected to allow her into those areas dear to cruising folk, and a full-lenth keel was selected for steadiness of handling, as well as the ability to haul out in small yards without cranes.

Because such a boat may entice her owner to Caribbean waters, special attention was paid to ventilation. She has four dorade vents. two flush-type vents, and five hatches and skylights. A coal stove provides for cabin comfort in northern waters.

The hull design incorporates a well-protected rudder in case of grounding. The lines show a pronounced bustle to reduce separation, and a fine entry for good performance from her tall ketch rig. A shorter rig is offered for heavy weather

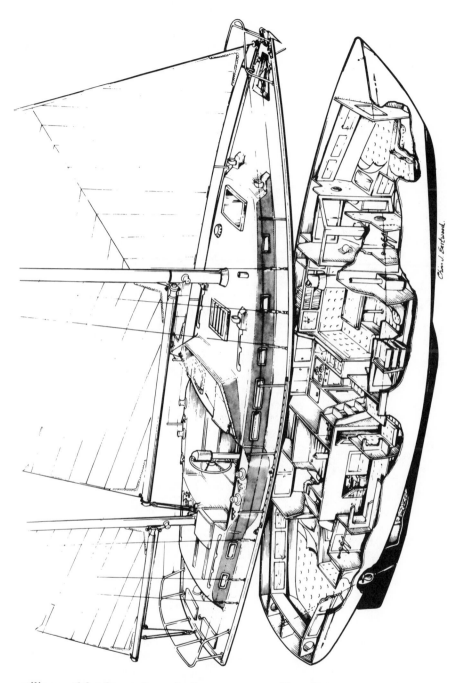

sailing, and for those who prefer less strenuous sailing. This boat is produced by Whitby Boat Works, 1710 Charles St., Whitby, Ont., Canada.

Hull and deck are fiberglass laminate, with balsa core in hull and deck; rig includes aluminum spars, stainless steel and dacron rigging, genoa furling gear and Barlow winches.

The standard arrangement accommodates 6-7; alternate layout includes star-

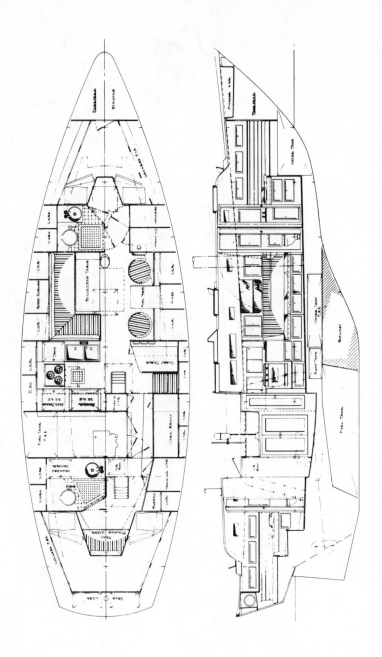

board berth in the saloon to sleep 7-8; both provide two toilet rooms with showers, large U-shaped galley, chart table, work bench, and generous stowage space.

The engine specified is a Perkins 4-107 or 4-236 diesel; fuel and water are 300 gallons each; electrical system is 12 VDC with 3.3 VAC generator on engine, dual batteries; there is a refrigerator and deep freeze.

Contact the builder for further information.

43-Ft. Cutter BLACK VELVET II

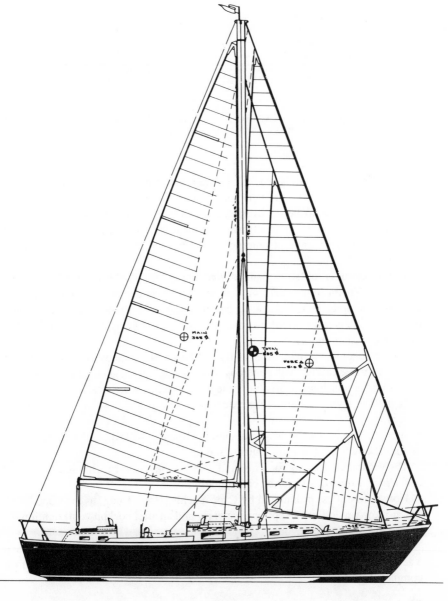

```
SPECIFICATIONS:
LOA.....................43'-2"
LWL....................35'-4"
BEAM...................12'-9"
DRAFT...................6'-4"
DISPL..............24,800 LBS
BALLAST............10,100 LBS
SAIL AREA...........895 SQ FT
POWER (DIESEL)........30-40 HP
FUEL..................90 GALS
WATER.................90 GALS
CONST (WOOD).......STRIP-PLANK
PRISMATIC COEFF......... .560
```

Black Velvet II was designed for an owner who wanted a fast, weatherly cruiser along modern lines. With her very long waterline, good stability, and ample sail area, she promises to be an excellent performer in all types of weather. Her prismatic coefficient is .56 (hull) which is ideal for high speeds. Along with this she has a very fine angle of entrance and a heavily developed bustle to reduce separation.

Construction is of strip-planked mahogany on bulkhead framing (polypropylene—Vectra—covered), with marine plywood decks and trunk. This is a strong-yet-simple method of custom building, giving low maintenance along with durability, and is within the ability of any small yard, or dedicated amateur builder. Spars are of aluminum.

The arrangement provides unusually good accommodations for up to 8 persons in three separate cabins, with generous stowage space throughout. Two large toilet rooms and a spacious, workable galley are fitted, as well as a large midship cockpit. The layout is perfect for extended cruising in any water, and for living aboard.

Auxiliary power can be any small diesel of about 30-40 HP, and with 90 gallons of fuel she will have a wide cruising radius.

The yachtsman looking for a fast and comfortable cruiser in this size range will find *Black Velvet II* worthy of consideration.

Now in fiberglass production by Cape Yachts, Hong Kong, as the Cape North 43, the new version has an optional yawl rig and an after cockpit configuration for those who prefer this layout.

Contact the designer for cost of study plans and construction blueprints, or Cape Yachts Ltd., P.O. Box 6, Peng Chau, N.T., Hong Kong, for information on completed yachts.

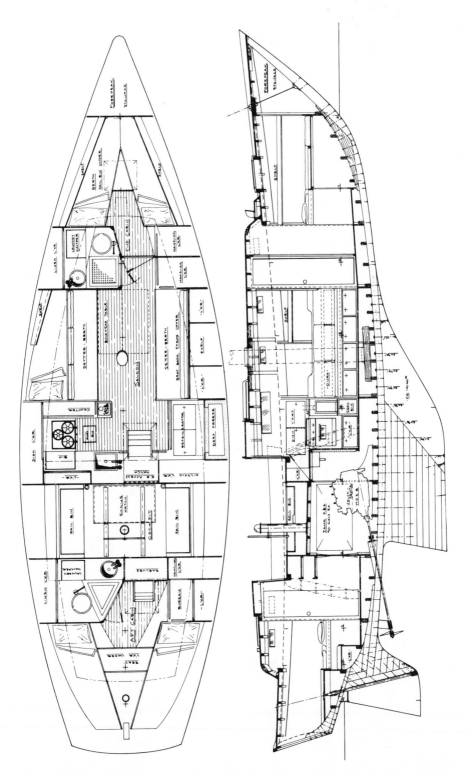

95

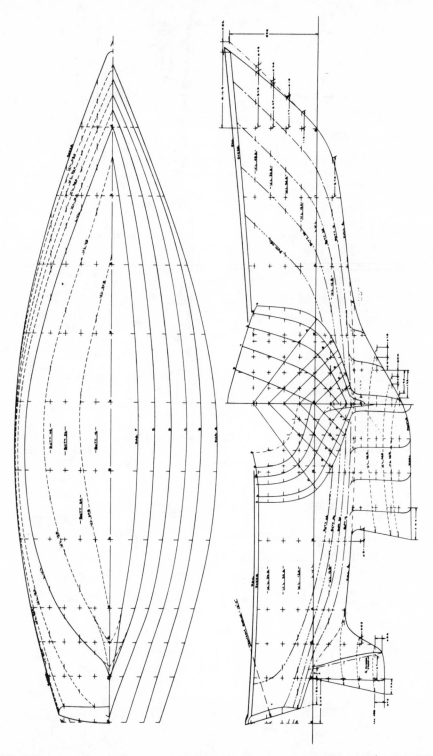

96

43-Ft. Yawl CAPE NORTH

SPECIFICATIONS:
```
LOA.................... 43'-2"
LWL.................... 35'-4"
BEAM.................. 12'-9"
DRAFT................. 6'-4"
DISPL............... 24,800 LBS
BALLAST............ 11,200 LBS
SAIL AREA (KETCH)..... 940 SQ FT
POWER (DIESEL)........... 35 HP
FUEL.................. 90 GALS
WATER................ 90 GALS
CONST............... FIBERGLASS
PRISMATIC COEFF.......    .56
```

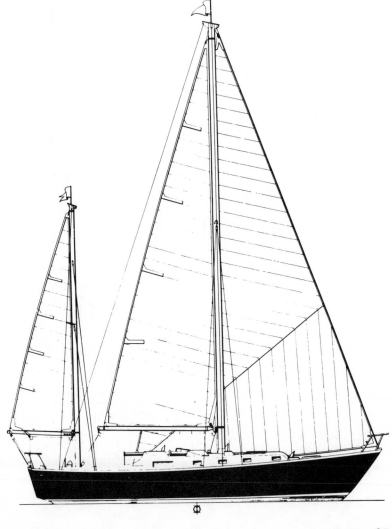

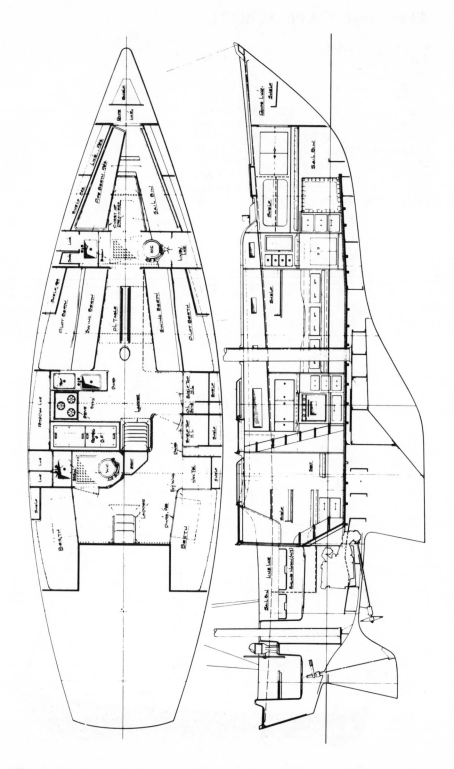

43-Ft. Ketch PACIFIC

```
SPECIFICATIONS:
LOA......................43'-6"
LOD......................41'-6"
LWL......................34'-8"
BEAM.....................13'-0"
DRAFT.....................6'-0"
DISPL................30,500 LBS
BALLAST (IRON).........9000 LBS
SAIL AREA.............954 SQ FT
POWER (GAS/DIESEL)......35-75 HP
FUEL...................180 GALS
WATER..................145 GALS
CONST (WOOD)..CARVEL/STRIP PLANK
PRISMATIC COEFF...........  .54
(Now in FRP production in Taiwan)
```

The *Pacific 42* was designed as a live-aboard auxiliary suitable for extended cruising in comfort. Her accommodations provide berths for seven persons in three separate cabins, or she can be laid out with a six-berth arrangement, plus a foc'sle workshop.

Construction is of conventional wood method — either carvel or strip planking on steam-bent frames. Decks may be fiberglass-covered marine plywood, or teak. The spars are spruce and detailed plans of the rig and fittings are included in the plans fee.

The hull has a prismatic coefficient of .54 for good performance under sail. The long keel assures a steady helm and allows the vessel to be hauled out easily for periodic scrubs and bottom paint at small, out-of-the-way yards that are so often used by cruising skippers.

Tank capacities are generous — 180 gallons of fuel and 145 gallons of water — allowing a wide crusing range. Auxiliary power may be diesel or gasoline, as preferred by the owner, in the 35 to 75 HP range. The Perkins 4-107 diesel produces excellent fuel economy, combined with reliability. Speeds with this engine will be about seven knots.

The first boat built to this design was — and may still be — owned by folk singer Burl Ives.

Contact the designer for cost of study plans and construction blueprints.

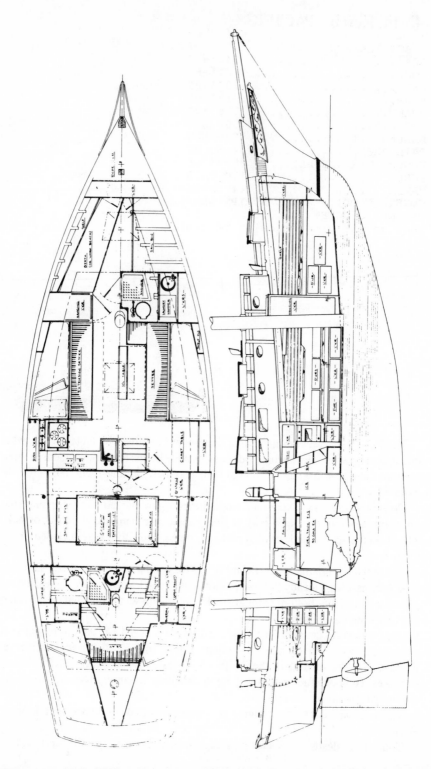

44-Ft. Ketch CAPE RACE

A husky diesel auxiliary of all steel-welded construction, *Cape Race* was designed for year-round live-aboard use and long-distance cruising.

Her accommodation plan is worthy of study as it features living quarters for 6-7 in three separate cabins, each with its own toilet room and shower. There is generous stowage space and ample tankage for extended voyaging — 300 gallons of water and 200 gallons of diesel fuel.

The first vessel built to this design was fitted with a 7 KW Onan generator, and has air conditioning, a deep freeze, electric refrigeration, warm-air heat, and many other conveniences.

The rig is simple and easily handled, with a roller-furling jib, and roller-reefing main and mizzen. The spars are set in tabernacles for ease of lowering in canal cruising, but this feature can be eliminated — at a saving — if not required.

Auxiliary power is by a Perkins or equal diesel of 70-80 HP for economical cruising speeds in the 7-knot range.

The original yacht built to this design, *Zig Zag,* has cruised the Baltic, the Mediterranean, and the canals of Holland, Belgium and France. Her owner reports that she is very comfortable, surprisingly fast under sail, and cruises under power easily at 7.5 to 8 knots.

Contact the designer for cost of study plans or construction blueprints.

SPECIFICATIONS:
```
LOA....................44'-1"
LWL....................37'-4"
BEAM...................14'-2"
DRAFT...................5'-0"
DISPL.............40,200 LBS
BALLAST.............7000 LBS
S/A (ALT RIGS).799-1000 SQ FT
POWER (DIESEL).......70-80 HP
FUEL................200 GALS
WATER...............300 GALS
CONST...........WELDED STEEL
PRISMATIC COEFF........ .558
```
(Also available as double
  chine hull for welded steel
  construction)

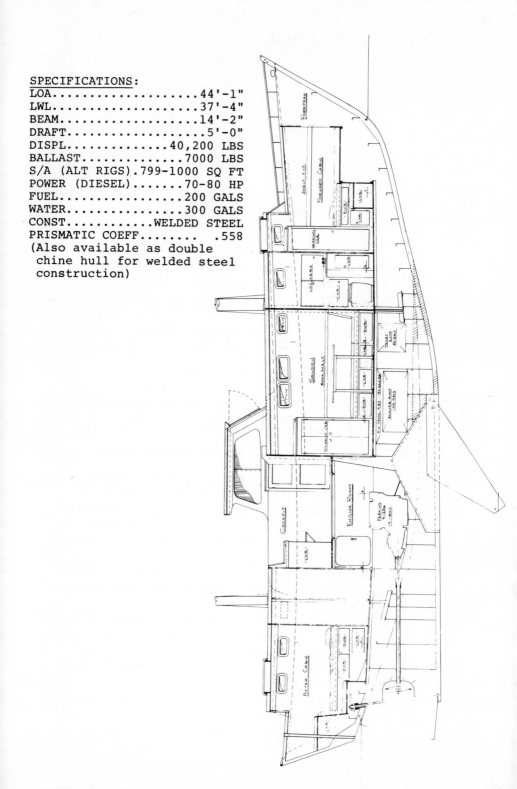

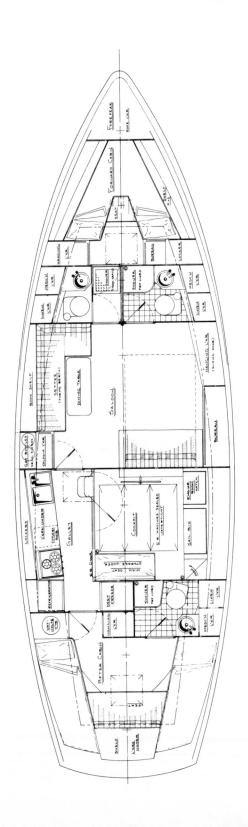

103

45-Ft. Pinky Schooner

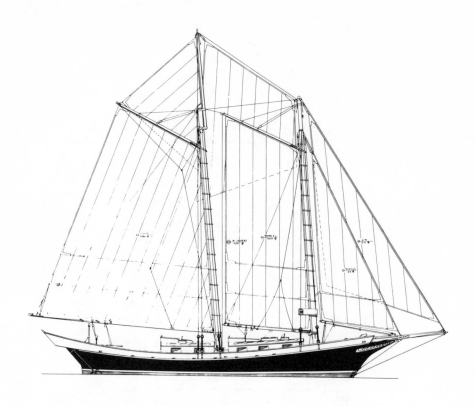

```
SPECIFICATIONS:
LOA.......................53'-9"
LOD.......................44'-9"
LWL.......................39'-0"
BEAM......................13'-5"
DRAFT.....................6'-3"
DISPL................45,000 LBS
BALLAST (OUTSIDE).......2700 LBS
BALLAST (INSIDE)......15,000 LBS
SAIL AREA.............1297 SQ FT
POWER (DIESEL)..........30-50 HP
FUEL....................80 GALS
WATER..................100 GALS
CONST (WOOD)........GLUED STRIP
PRISMATIC COEFF...........  .56
```

Designed for Penobscot Boat Works of Rockport, Maine, this husky pinky schooner is modelled after *Dove*, a fishing schooner built in Nova Scotia in the 1800's. Changes from the original design include a finer hull, a slight increase in freeboard, a modified rudder, double headsails with main topsail; and, the fish

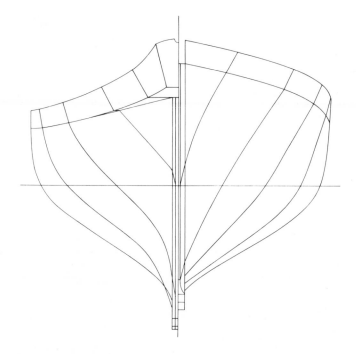

hold has given way to more commodious accommodations below.

The arrangement shows berths for eight in two double and four single berths. An alternative plan for the dining area shows a pilot berth and a single settee berth in place of the double berth formed by the table. This arrangement will be used in the first boat now building for a Boston owner and should prove quite comfortable.

The schooner will be outfitted and handled as traditionally as possible, with a minimum of winches and other fancy gear. There is no wheel steering, electric refrigeration, electric windlass, pressure water system or hot water tank, and navigation equipment will be kept to a minimum. Wood shell blocks, deadeyes, brains and muscle will replace most of the gadgets considered essential today.

Launching is scheduled for the summer of 1975 but, to date, no name has been selected. She is certainly going to attract much interest in any port she enters and, yes, Virginia, the pinky stern *is* intended to be used as an auxiliary head, just as the fishermen did with it 100 years ago.

Contact the designer for cost of study plans or construction blueprints, or Penobscot Boat Works, Rockport, ME 04856, for data on completed craft.

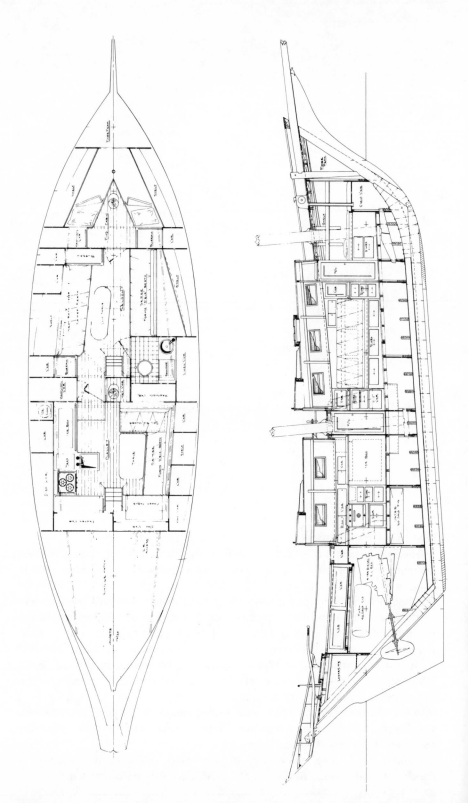

47-Ft. Ketch OLYMPIC ADVENTURE

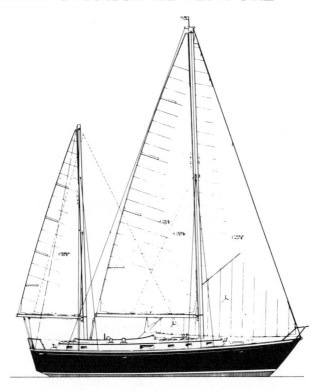

The *Olympic Adventure 47* was designed to provide a comfortable live-aboard auxiliary cruiser. The hull form is that of a pure sailing yacht with firm bilges, a well-developed bustle, and a fine entrance; however, the husky auxiliary engine will drive this hull at motor-sailer speeds under power.

The rig spreads ample sail area to move her well in any weather, and a double-headsail arrangement with boomed staysail is optional for those preferring such a set-up.

The accommodations provide for 6-8 berths for the owner's party, if required, in three separate cabins, and one or two crew berths in a private cabin. There are two toilet rooms with showers in each for owner and guests, plus optional head and basin for crew.

The engine is a Volvo-Penta 100 HP diesel with 2:1 RG. Fuel totals 175 gallons in two tanks, water 300 gallons in two tanks. The optional holding tank has a 50-gallon capacity. There is a 3 KW auxiliary generator, plus refrigerator and deep-freeze.

Spars are aluminum with roller reefing. Rigging will be of stainless steel wire and dacron rope. Winches are by Barlow. Contact Olympic Yachts S.A., Zea Marina, Piraeus Greece, or Steve Colgate Sailing Enterprises, 820 Second Ave., New York, N.Y. 10017, for further information on this yacht and the new Olympic Adventure 42.

```
SPECIFICATIONS:
LOA.....................47'-0"
LWL.....................38'-0'
BEAM....................14'-3"
DRAFT...................5'-10"
DISPL...............30,000 LBS
BALLAST.............11,000 LBS
SAIL AREA...........1057 SQ FT
POWER (DIESEL)..........100 HP
FUEL.................175 GALS
WATER................300 GALS
CONST...............FIBERGLASS
PRISMATIC COEFF.......... .54
```

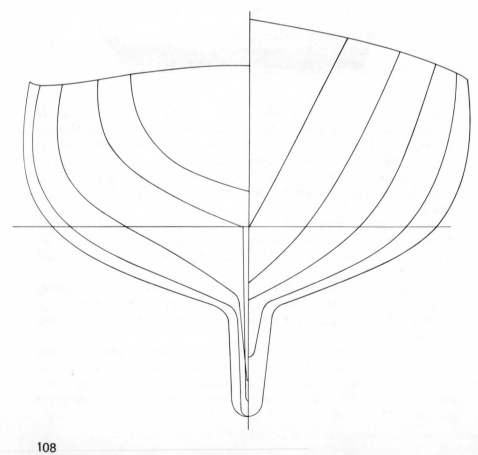

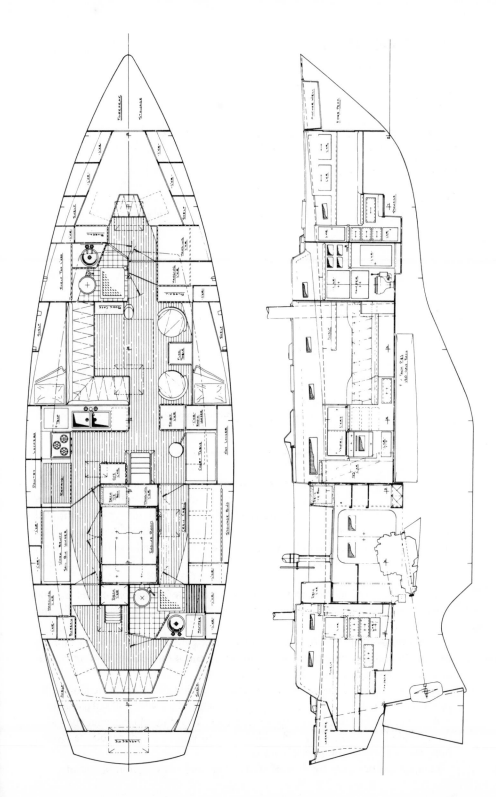

51-Ft. Yawl JULIE

SPECIFICATIONS:

```
LOA....................51'-0"
LWL...................36'-11"
BEAM..................13'-1"
DRAFT..................6'-0"
DISPL..............37,000 LBS
BALLAST (LEAD).....12,000 LBS
SAIL AREA......... 1120 SQ FT
POWER (2 DIESELS).EA 50-70 HP
FUEL.................200 GALS
WATER...............340 GALS
CONST.............FIBERGLASS
```

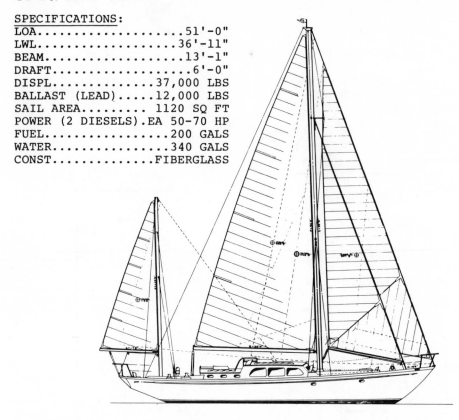

Julie is a fine, twin-screw cruising yawl, an excellent example of a one-off custom design, and of the finish that can be achieved in fiberglass construction using an existing mold. Tyler of England modified the hull, giving it a traditional long counter, a new skeg and rudder, and six inches less draft than the original Hood 50 hull. The deck mold was modified byTyler to conform to our designs; cabin trunks were fabricated of wood, nylon covered for durability and ease of maintenance.

Tanks were modified during hull molding to provide 200 gallons of fuel and 300 of water, and engine beds were modified to take twin Osco 172 diesels. Feathering propellers are. fitted.

The arrangement is truly commodious, sleeping 8 in three cabins. Comforts include: two large toilet rooms with showers, central oil heat, electric refrigeration, and a roomy saloon with coal-fired heater.

Aluminum spars, Lewmar winches, and an ample sail area provide a powerful yet easily handled double-headsail rig. The owner and his wife will sail alone most of the time, and will live aboard for long periods. Thus, a yacht that could be sailed short-handed was essential, and with twin-screw power and double headsails, *Julie* meets their requirements handsomely.

Contact the designer for cost of study plans and construction blueprints.

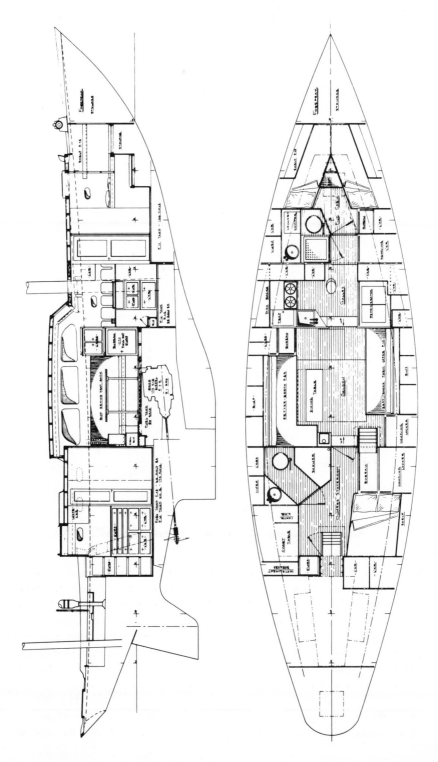

111

54-Ft. Ketch ENTERPRISE

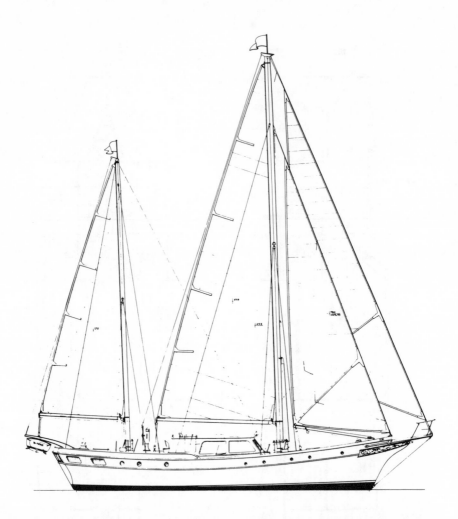

Enterprise is an ocean-going auxiliary yacht designed for extended voyaging in comfort. The design is based on our successful *Mystic* (a welded aluminum yacht of similar size), but the displacement and sail area have been increased to compensate for wood construction.

While construction is of wood, she is sturdily built to solid scantling rules, and takes advantage of modern triple-diagonal planking to reduce maintenance, eliminate caulking and ensure more than adequate strength. With normal care a wood hull of this type should last 50 years or more.

Rig and spars are of stainless steel and aluminum for strength and lightness. The tall, efficient rig spreads ample sail area for fast performance under all conditions and, indeed, *Mystic* placed second in her class in the 1969 Trans-Pac race.

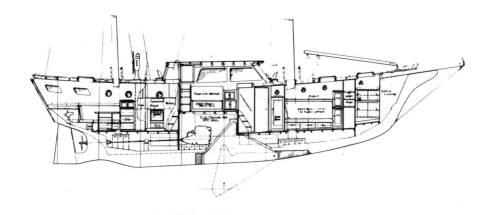

```
SPECIFICATIONS:
LOA.....................53'-11"
LWL.....................47'-0"
BEAM....................16'-3"
DRAFT (bd dn 10').......6'-0"
DISPL..............70,000 LBS
BALLAST (LEAD).....16,000 LBS
SAIL AREA..........1523 SQ FT
POWER (DIESEL).......50-80 HP
FUEL.................500 GALS
WATER................300 GALS
CONST......TRIPLE-DIAG CARVEL
PRISMATIC COEFF.......   .57
```

Through a cruiser, and a comfortable one, *Enterprise* will not be slow.

Auxiliary power is diesel, and engines of 60-80 HP continuous shaft HP may be fitted for good cruising speeds with fuel economy. Fuel tankage of 500 gallons provides a good range.

The arrangement provides six berths in two or three separate cabins. A fourth two-berth crew or guest cabin could be fitted instead of the ship's office. In addition to the double berth the great cabin also provides two sea berths. An athwartship double berth, while comfortable in port, rarely is at sea in rough weather.

The great cabin plus a large saloon-pilothouse provides generous seating space, while wide, uncluttered decks provide ideal lounging space for the off-watch crew.

With the possibility of chartering in mind, her layout is ideal, as it can provide for 4-6 guests forward, with the owner-captain living aft, where the galley is also located.

In sum, *Enterprise* is a fast and comfortable long-distance cruiser, equally suited to island hopping in the Caribbean, a trans-Atlantic passage, or a circumnavigation if the owner is so inclined.

Contact the designer for price of study plans or construction blueprints.

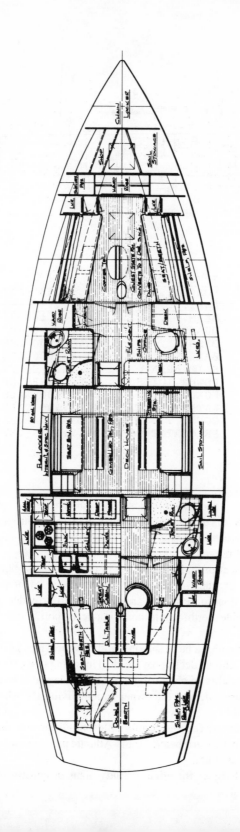

114

56-Ft. Schooner MYSTIC

```
SPECIFICATIONS:
LOA.....................55'-9"
LWL.....................46'-9"
BEAM....................15'-0"
DRAFT (BD DN 8'-9".......6'-0"
DISPL..............53,800 LBS
BALLAST............14,000 LBS
SAIL AREA..........1403 SQ FT
POWER (DIESEL).........170 HP
FUEL.................950 GALS
WATER...............450 GALS
CONST...............ALUMINUM
PRISMATIC COEFF.......... .57
```

Mystic was designed to replace a smaller, heavier yacht of similar type. The client wanted better performance under sail, yet the room and comfort of the earlier vessel. For this reason and for durability, the hull was designed for aluminum construction — giving strength with extreme lightness so that a finer hull with better sailing characteristics would result. Normally, a vessel of this size would be planked with 1½" to 1⅜" mahogany. The heaviest aluminum plates weigh only as much as 1⅛" mahogany, a saving of about 20% in weight over a wood yacht. Compared to a steel yacht with $^3/_{16}$" plate, the ¼" aluminum produces a weight saving of over 100%.

Mystic carries only six tons of ballast (a low 22% ratio), but her deep oil and water tanks add another 3½ tons of weight down in the keel to provide ample stability.

Her accomodations include an owner's cabin aft sleeping 2-4 with private toilet room. There is a large forward cabin for guests, sleeping 2-4, which canconvert to two double cabins — with toilet room and shower. There is also a crew cabin with toilet and basin. The joiner work is of teak.

Spars are aluminum; rigging is stainless steel wire and dacron rope; sails are dacron; the hull plating calls for $^3/_{16}$" and ¼" plate on 2" x $^3/_{16}$" frames on 14" centers.

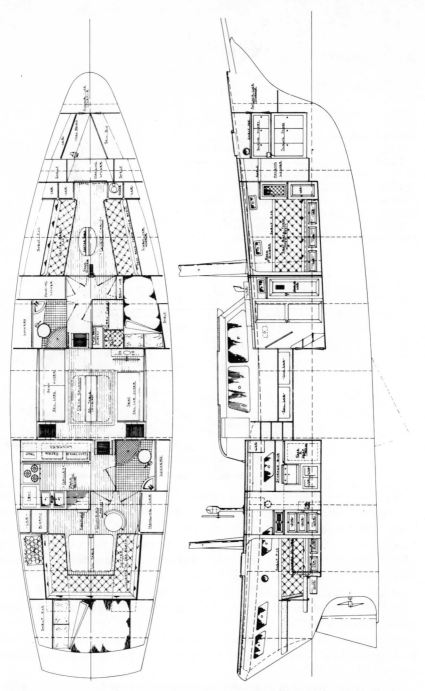

For power, *Mystic* has a Caterpillar diesel of 170 HP with 2:1 RG. She carries 950 gallons of fuel and 450 gallons of water. Cruising speed is eight knots. The refrigerator and deep freeze are by Grunert. Steering is Warner hydraulic with a Wood-Freeman auto-pilot. The electrical system is 32-volt with two 300 AH batteries.

Contact the designer for price of study plans and construction blueprints.

116

61-Ft. Ketch TRAVELLER III

SPECIFICATIONS:
```
LOA.....................62'-2"
LWL.....................48'-0"
BEAM....................16'-1"
DRAFT....................6'-0"
DISPL...............71,000 Lbs
BALLAST (LEAD)......18,000 LBS
SAIL AREA...........1789 SQ FT
POWER (DIESEL).......70-120 HP
FUEL..................250 GALS
WATER.................300 GALS
CONST (DOUBLE).....CARVEL WOOD
PRISMATIC COEFF.......... .565
```

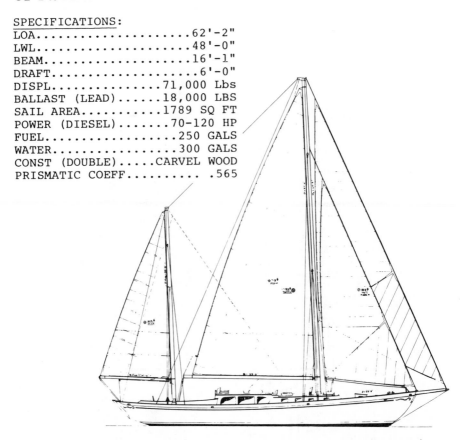

Traveller III was designed for a well-known charter boat owner whose requirements were shaped after years of experience on craft of all sizes.

Accommodations are provided for an owner's party of 6-7 in three cabins, plus a hand forward. A large deep freeze and refrigerator are fitted, along with sufficient tankage for long periods at sea. She carries 400 gallons of water and 250 gallons of fuel. The saloon is air conditioned for comfort in the tropics. The auxiliary engine is a GM 4-71 diesel, and an Onan 7 KW generator provides electric power.

Construction is of the highest quality: double-planked teak, bronze fastened, with teak decks and trim. The centerboard, centerboard trunk, mast steps and engine beds all are heavy bronze for strength and durability.

The seaworthy ketch rig spreads a good area of sail for the desired performance in light-weather conditions, and will balance nicely under a fairly wide variety of sail combinations for comfort and control in heavy weather conditions.

With her spacious saloon and roomy cockpit, *Traveller III* should provide the kind of comfort, luxury and performance demanded by many charter parties and be a first-class home afloat for the charter captain and his crew.

For more information, or prices of study plans and cost of construction blueprints, contact the designer directly.

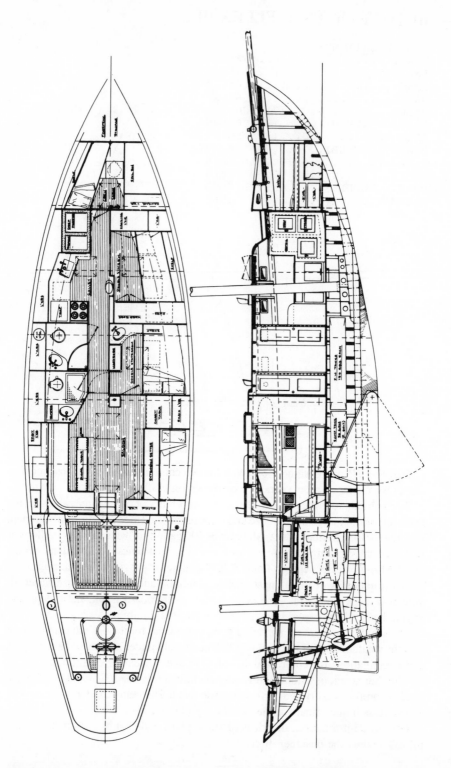

A Portfolio
of Brewer Boats

Cape Carib Ketch (page 57).

Grand Banks 28 (page 54).   *Aloha 28 (page 52).*

Schooner Spanish Main (Plans not shown. Photo: Reg Lewis)

Chappaquiddick 25 Catboat (page 45).

Traveller III (page 119).   *Olympic Adventure (page 107).*   **121**

Aluminum frames stacked up for Mystic Ketch (page 67).

Jason Cutter under construction (page 77).

Mercury Express Cruiser (plans not shown).

Half Model of MB/S 35 (page 80).

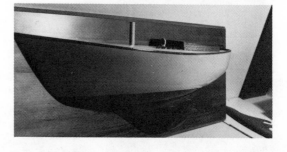

Powerboats

18-Ft. O/B Cruiser HERRICK BAY 18

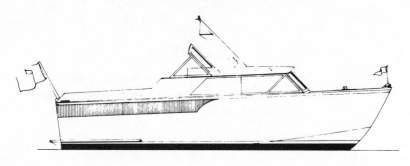

```
SPECIFICATIONS:
LOA.....................18'-0"
LWL.....................15'-5"
BEAM....................7'-10"
DRAFT...................0'-9"
DISPL...................1810 LBS
POWER (O/B)...........40-100 HP
HEADROOM................4'-4"
FUEL................6-12 GALS
WATER..................20 GALS
CONST..........MARINE PLYWOOD
```

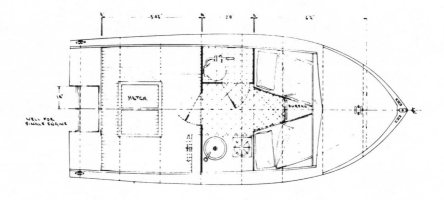

These two outboard cruisers, the *Herrick Bay 18* and *Herrick Bay 20,* are two versions of the same hull, the larger model offering more comfort in its accommodations.

Designed as simple-to-build cruisers for the backyard boat-builder, both have marine plywood planking and decks and are glued and nail-fastened for strength, tightness and ease of construction. Bulkhead framing eliminates the usual large number of sawn frames.

Excellent accommodations are shown for boats this size. The 18-footer sleeps

20-Ft. O/B Cruiser HERRICK BAY 20

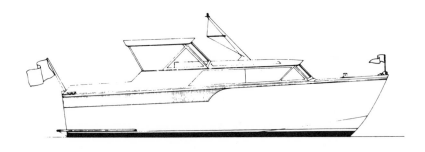

SPECIFICATIONS:
```
LOA......................20'-0"
LWL......................17'-4"
BEAM.....................7'-10"
DRAFT....................0'-9"
DISPL..................2200 LBS
POWER (O/B)...........40-100 HP
HEADROOM.................4'-7"
FUEL................12-20 GALS
WATER..................20 GALS
CONST............MARINE PLYWOOD
```

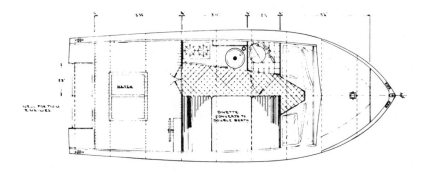

two with a galley and enclosed toilet. The 20-footer sleeps four—two in the forward V-berths, and two more in the convertible dinette. This model also has an enclosed head and a galley. Cabin headroom in the 18-footer is 4'-4", and in the 20-footer, it is 4'-7", ample for comfortable sitting and relaxing in both cases.

Power for the two boats offers a wide range of choices. A 40 HP outboard will produce speeds up to 18 MPH, and 100 HP will produce speeds of over 25 MPH. Single or twin outboard installations can be used.

Contact the designer for cost of study plans or large size construction blueprints.

24-Ft. Sport Cruiser or Day Cruiser FLYE POINT 24

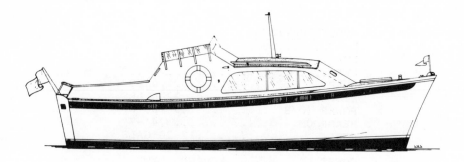

Designed for the owner who wants an economical and practical cruiser, the *Flye Point 24* is seaworthy enough for offshore fishing.

She is available in two versions, either as a day cruiser with a shelter top, or as an out-and-out family cruiser. The day cruiser has two berths forward and a toilet so it can be used for weekend cruising. The full cruiser version has two forward berths, a settee convertible to a double berth, an enclosed toilet, and complete galley — providing full cruising comforts for vacation trips.

Either version could be fitted out as a seaworthy small sportsfisherman with the addition of rod holders and fighting chairs.

Construction is of Philippine mahogany seam-batten planking, on sawn white oak frames, marine plywood decks and a mahogany cabin with teak or mahogany trim. She is bronze-screw fastened, and sturdy enough to last a lifetime.

The hull lines carry the flare from bow to stern, insuring a dry boat under all normal sea conditions, while her generous beam will contribute markedly to stability and seaworthiness. The hull design reduces pounding in a seaway to a minimum, and permits fast cruising — with comfort — in choppy seas.

Power is provided by a pair of Universal Unimite Fours of 70 HP each — or engines of equal power — and this installation will produce excellent speeds, enough to meet the requirements of most owners. These engines are lightweight, economical and reliable, and yet are small enough to permit a neat installation under a flush cockpit deck — allowing use of deck chairs and an outside table at anchor or when docked.

Contact the designer directly for information regarding price of small study plans or large-scale construction blueprints.

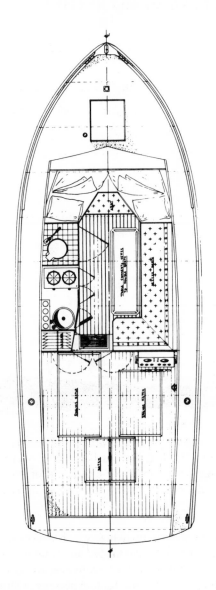

SPECIFICATIONS:
```
LOA......................24'-3"
LWL......................21'-8"
BEAM......................9'-0"
DRAFT.....................2'-0"
DISPL..................5000 LBS
POWER (2 GAS)........EACH 70 HP
FUEL...................40 GALS
WATER..................18 GALS
CONST.........SEAM-BATTEN CARVEL
```

27-Ft. Weekend Cruiser BLUE HILL

```
SPECIFICATIONS:
LOA......................27'-3"
LWL......................25'-0"
BEAM......................9'-1"
DRAFT.....................2'-4"
DISPL..................5700 LBS
POWER (GAS OR DIESEL)..TO 120 HP
FUEL....................60 GALS
WATER...................30 GALS
CONST............FRP OVER PLANK
```

Blue Hill is a design suited to a wide variety of uses: day cruiser, weekender, fishing boat, or utility. Her hull form is based on a successful 20-footer, and insures excellent rough-water ability at either low or high speeds. The sharp entrance of her bow reduces pounding and the double-ended hull assures freedom from yawing in following seas, with an added bonus of low-speed efficiency when trolling.

Construction is of cedar strip-planking, which is covered with fiberglass for reduced maintenance and added strength. The hull employs bulkhead framing, and the keel, is laminated to provide extra longitudinal strength.

The accommodations provide berths for four persons, with an enclosed head and a useful galley.

Power may be either gasoline or diesel, single screw, to a top of about 200 HP, which will produce speeds of over 20 knots, if desired. A V-drive places the engine aft, reducing the noise level in the cabin.

Twin steering stations provide the helmsman with real steering comfort in either good weather or bad, and mark the vessel as suited to all-purpose, all-weather use. At this size, she is a type that will please many owners who are looking for a boat in the mid-range.

Contact the designer for cost of study plans or large-scale blueprints.

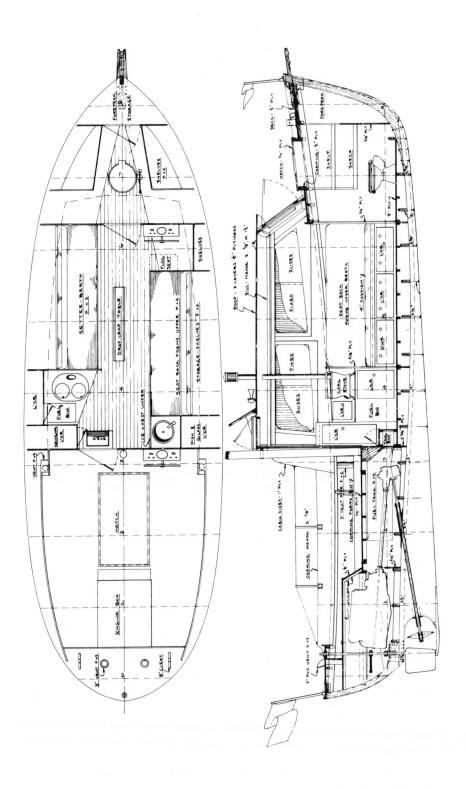

28-Ft. Cruiser DEER ISLE

SPECIFICATIONS:
```
LOA.....................28'-2"
LWL.....................24'-8"
BEAM.....................9'-6"
DRAFT...................1'-10"
DISPL................6500 LBS
POWER (1 or 2 I/O)...to 300 HP
FUEL..................70 GALS
WATER.................20 GALS
CONST..............MARINE PLY
PRISMATIC COEFF........ .728
```

Designed to offer the lobsterman or amateur builder an economical vessel, simple to build and maintain, and with excellent sea-keeping ability, the *Deer Isle 28* will do double duty as a workboat, yard tender, sportfishermen, day cruiser, or cruiser.

Construction calls for marine plywood planking, ⅝" on the topsides and ¾" on the bottom, on longitudinal framing — which is ideal for the backyard builder due to the simplicity of this planking technique. Fastenings for the hull structure are bronze bolts and bronze Anchorfast nails are used to attach the planking.

Single or twin outdrive engines can be used, to a total of 300 HP — with really flashing speed performance at the upper end of the horsepower scale. NOTE: The after-cabin cruiser will only take a single engine. The working lobsterman will appreciate the versatility of the outdrive engine when he is maneuvering in close quarters to reach his pot buoys, or untangling the pot warp from his propeller. A single 150 HP outdrive engine will push her to over 20 knots, and let her cruise at 15-16 knots with good economy.

The accommodation plan shows a nice privacy in the double-cabin version, with

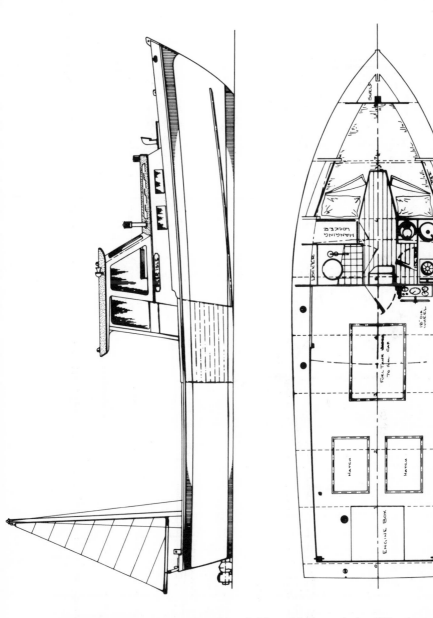

a complete galley and an enclosed head. The midship cockpit will be dry and safe in heavy weather.

This is a boat that is simple to build — saving cost — and will prove to be fast, comfortable and inexpensive to operate — earning her keep again and again in pleasure and utility for the owner who appreciates her virtues.

Contact the designer directly for cost of study plans and large-scale blueprints.

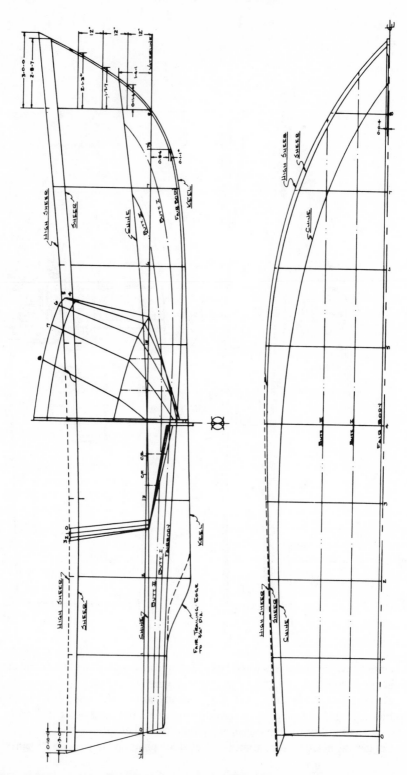

32-Ft. Cruiser DRAGON LADY

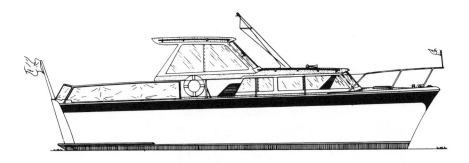

The 32-foot cruiser *Dragon Lady* is a seaworthy, round-bilge cruiser providing excellent accommodations for 4 to 6 persons, including complete galley facilities, an enclosed toilet with shower, and generous stowage space. The hull is a seakindly one, and owners report that she is soft-riding in rough water conditions.

Construction is robust, consisting of teak and mahogany planking on steam-bent white oak frames, with teak or marine plywood decks, a mahogany or teak cabin and trim. Fastenings are bronze screws. The keel and stem are of white oak.

Power may be single or twin gasoline or diesel engines producing up to about 400 HP. In the first boat built from this design, a pair of Universal Knights proved to be an excellent choice, providing speed, economy, and reliability.

The tankage provides capacity for 100 gallons of fuel, and 100 gallons of water. The tanks are of stainless steel, as are the propeller and other important metal parts, in order to eliminate corrosion.

The hull is an easily driven one, and will reach 16 MPH with a single 140 HP engine. Additional power can be selected to achieve speeds to 30 MPH, if desired.

The roomy cockpit enables the fisherman to use his boat as a sportfisherman by adding rod holders and fighting chairs. The beamy hull assures ample stability for landing large fish over the cockpit sides or transom.

A 35-foot version of this design, with a longer cockpit and twin outdrive engines mounted in the stern, is also available.

Contact the designer for cost of study plans or blueprints.

```
SPECIFICATIONS:
LOA.....................32'-0"
LWL.....................28'-0"
BEAM....................11'-0"
DRAFT....................2'-7"
DISPL.................9000 LBS
POWER (1/2,G or D)...to 400 HP
FUEL.................220 GALS
WATER................100 GALS
CONST (WOOD)...........CARVEL
PRISMATIC COEFF........  .714
```

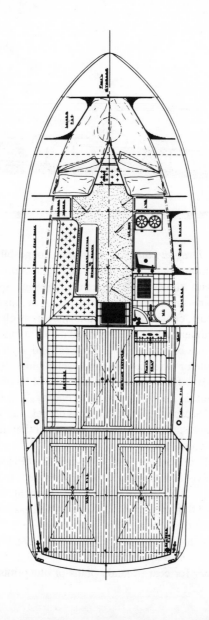

33-Ft. Cruiser GRAND BANKS

SPECIFICATIONS:
```
LOA..................32'-9"
LWL..................30'-8"
BEAM.................10'-0"
DRAFT................3'-9"
DISPL.............20,000 LBS
POWER...............40-60 HP
FUEL................250 GALS
WATER...............100 GALS
CONST...FRP OVER GLUED-STRIP
STEADYING RIG.......88 SQ FT
```

The *Grand Banks 33* is a husky offshore cruiser suited to extended voyages in Southern or Northern waters. Her economical diesel engine gives her a cruising range of 500 miles. A vessel of this type is not limited to short dashes from port to port, but can remain offshore running night and day if required, churning out 150-200 miles under her keel every 24 hours. She is ideal for living aboard for long periods, or permanently.

Construction is staunch in keeping with her type, but has been developed with simplicity in mind so that the small yard or competant home builder will be able to handle her. Bulkhead framing is employed to eliminate steam-bent frames, and the planking is glued-strip construction, fiberglass- or dynel-covered for tightness and minimum maintenance. Decks are laid white pine, left bare for good footing on wet days.

The small steadying rig of 88 sq. ft. will be useful in reducing rolling, and will enable her to reach downwind port in the event of engine trouble. The boom is long enough to serve as a dinghy hoist so the dink can be stowed in the cockpit while running, thus eliminating the nuisance — and occasional danger — of towing it.

Contact the designer for cost of study plans or blueprints.

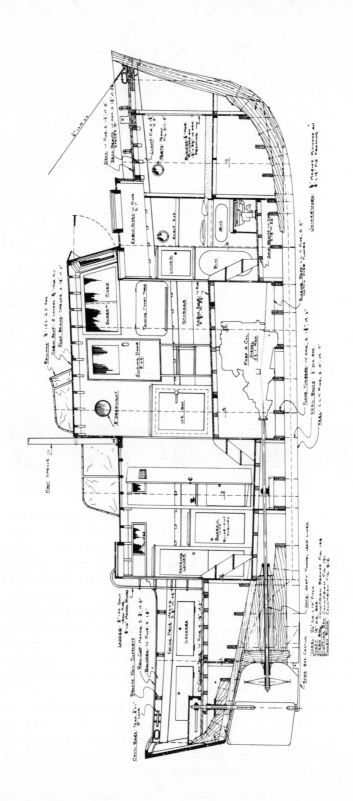

136

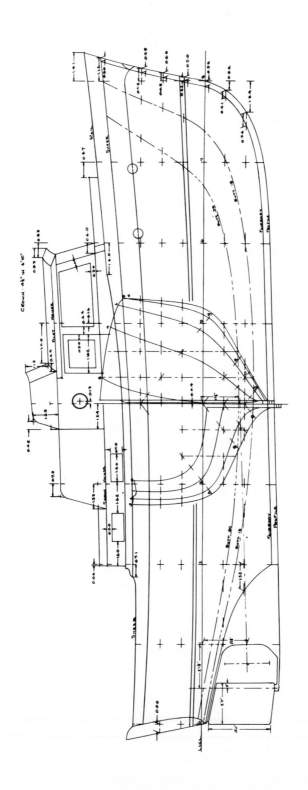

137

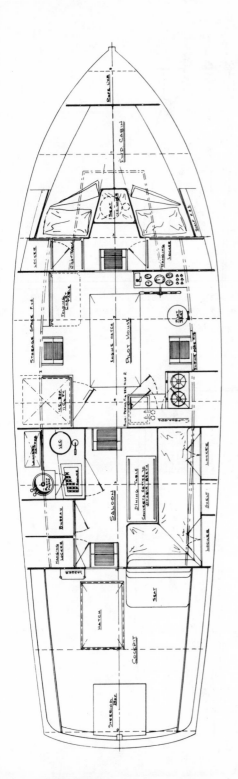

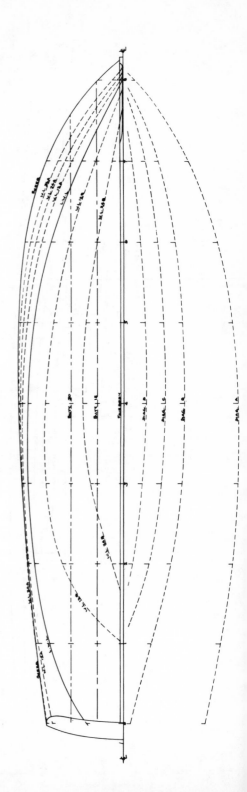

37-Ft. Cruiser DEER ISLE

```
SPECIFICATIONS:
LOA....................36'-9"
LWL....................34'-1"
BEAM...................12'-0"
DRAFT...................3'-8"
DISPL..............19,000 LBS
POWER (1 or 2 dsl)...75-160 HP
FUEL..................180 GALS
WATER.................150 GALS
CONST.......SEAM-BATTEN CARVEL
```

A husky, 37-foot cruiser designed for live-aboard comfort, operating economy, and seaworthiness, the *Deer Isle 37* was designed for seam-batten carvel planking on heavy sawn frames — providing ease of construction, durability, and a tight hull without the need for caulking. Small boatyards or competent backyard builders will find few difficulties in building her.

Decks and cabin trunk are of marine plywood, vectra- or fiberglass-covered to insure a tight job and reduce maintenance. Power is a single gas or diesel engine of 75-160 HP, or twin engines each 75-100 HP. Fuel capacity of 180 gallons, and water tankage of 150 gallons permit a long operating range. A steadying rig may be fitted, and plans for this are included in the plans set.

Berths for five are provided, in three cabins, and a sixth is possible. Galley and toilet facilities are complete, and there is generous storage space throughout.

The yachtsman who requires a live-aboard coastal cruiser will find this vessel an excellent choice for this purpose.

Contact designer for cost of study plans or blueprints.

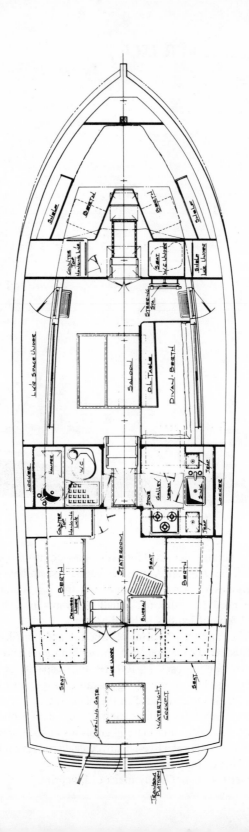

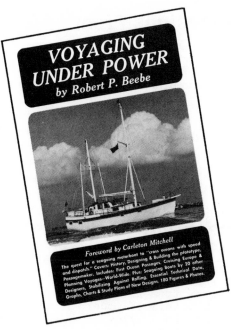

"A boating book whose time has come..."

As the early reviews below reveal, here's a book whose time has come! One which truly widens motorboat cruising horizons. It's the story of Capt. Robert P. Beebe's quest for a new type of motorboat capable of crossing oceans & also serving as a full-time live-aboard home for a family. Includes boat designs by 20 other famous U.S. designers. Plus chapters on: Voyage Planning, Stabilizing Against Rolling, Galley Tips. Also: 180 Figures & Photos. Hard Cover. Cloth Bound. 272 p.

$12.90 PPD.

What The Reviewers Say

"It's sound, attractive, sensible; and libraries will have a demand for it."   --Library Journal

"We heartily recommend it to anyone, power or sail."
                    --Nor'Westing Magazine

"A definitive book..."   --Yachting Magazine

"Worth the price for...do-it-yourself boatmakers."
                    --THE ENSIGN (USPS Magazine)

"There is no other book like it."   --Nat'l Fisherman

"...as carefully and expertly thought out as Hiscock's Voyaging Under Sail."   --Tony Gibbs, USCG Aux.

"...a book whose time has come. This book is a must."
                    --Carleton Mitchell, Sailor/Author

"Robert Beebe has produced...a fine book...for motorboat cruising men."   --Motorboat Magazine

"Everything You Always Wanted To Know About Seagoing Motorboats But Didn't Know Whom To Ask." --Down East

THE DESIGNER'S SERIES

17 Designs From the Board of John G. Hanna

17 study plans of John Hanna's famous double-ended ketches--inclu-the 30' TAHITI--with specs and photos, and source & price of plans.

32 Designs From the Board of Al Mason

A master draftsman of-fers 32 cruising boat designs from 20 to 53 feet, with both modern & traditional rigs, for cruising & racing.

20 Designs From the Board of Thomas E. Colvin

A collection of "ocean sailing cruising ves-sels" and shoal-draft sharpies in varied sizes & rigs for wood, steel and ferro-cement.

Conversation with A World Voyager

Tale of a 7-year, 63,000-mile voyage around the world in a home-built steel ketch <u>White Seal</u>. Stressing simplicity, the Question-and-Answer format makes this book a handy manual of useful tips and techniques for those who love cruising.

FOR PRICES, PLEASE SEND FOR OUR LATEST PUBLISHER'S LOG

Cruising Designs From the Board of Winthrop L. Warner

A superb collection of 26 cruising boat designs for wood construction. Sizes from 13' to 46'. Includes high performance types and heavy cruising auxiliaries

Cruising Designs From the Board of Thomas C. Gillmer

Cruising boat designs of conventional and modern rig and underbody by the designer of the 30' SEAWIND, 1st fiberglass circumnavigator.

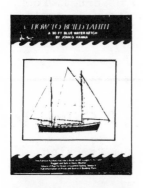

How-To-Build Tahiti

Complete building instructions for John Hanna's most famous double-ended ketch, 30' TAHITI. A rugged deep-water vessel, safe in heavy weather. Four berths. Choice of coastwise or ocean-going rigs. Source and price of plans included.

How-To-Build Gulfweed

John Hanna's simple chine hull for the backyard builder. Rig: Schooner, Ketch or Sloop. Two cockpit layouts. Three keel versions: 28" C/B model, 38" intermediate keel, 48" deep keel for ocean work. Source and price of plans included.

FOR PRICES, PLEASE SEND FOR
OUR LATEST PUBLISHER'S LOG